Better Learning

THROUGH STRUCTURED TEACHING

ASCD MEMBER BOOK

Many ASCD members received this book as a member benefit upon its initial release.

Learn more at: **www.ascd.org/memberbooks**

Better
Learning

**THROUGH
STRUCTURED
TEACHING**

A Framework for the Gradual
Release of Responsibility

Douglas Fisher | Nancy Frey

Association for Supervision and Curriculum Development
Alexandria, Virginia USA

Association for Supervision and Curriculum Development
1703 N. Beauregard St. • Alexandria, VA 22311-1714 USA
Phone: 800-933-2723 or 703-578-9600 • Fax: 703-575-5400
Web site: www.ascd.org • E-mail: member@ascd.org
Author guidelines: www.ascd.org/write

Gene R. Carter, *Executive Director;* Nancy Modrak, *Director of Publishing;* Julie Houtz, *Director of Book Editing & Production;* Deborah Siegel, *Project Manager;* Catherine Guyer, *Senior Graphic Designer;* Marlene Hochberg, *Typesetter;* Sarah Plumb, *Production Specialist*

Printed in the United States of America. Cover art copyright © 2008 by ASCD. ASCD publications present a variety of viewpoints. The views expressed or implied in this book should not be interpreted as official positions of the Association.

All Web links in this book are correct as of the publication date below but may have become inactive or otherwise modified since that time. If you notice a deactivated or changed link, please e-mail books@ascd.org with the words "Link Update" in the subject line. In your message, please specify the Web link, the book title, and the page number on which the link appears.

ASCD Member Book, No. FY08-5 (February 2008, P). ASCD Member Books mail to Premium (P) and Comprehensive (C) members on this schedule: Jan., PC; Feb., P; Apr., PC; May, P; July, PC; Aug., P; Sept., PC; Nov., PC; Dec., P.

PAPERBACK ISBN: 978-1-4166-0635-2   ASCD product #108010
Also available as an e-book through ebrary, netLibrary, and many online booksellers (see Books in Print for the ISBNs).

Quantity discounts for the paperback edition only: 10–49 copies, 10%; 50+ copies, 15%; for 1,000 or more copies, call 800-933-2723, ext. 5634, or 703-575-5634. For desk copies: member@ascd.org.

Library of Congress Cataloging-in-Publication Data

Fisher, Douglas, 1965-
  Better learning through structured teaching : a framework for the gradual release of responsibility / Douglas Fisher and Nancy Frey.
     p. cm.
  Includes bibliographical references and index.
  ISBN 978-1-4166-0635-2 (pbk. : alk. paper) 1. Active learning. 2. Teaching. 3. Constructivism (Education) I. Frey, Nancy, 1959- II. Title.

  LB1027.23.F56 2008
  371.39–dc22

                                2007040586

18 17 16 15 14 13 12 11 10 09 08 07   1 2 3 4 5 6 7 8 9 10 11 12

Better Learning

THROUGH STRUCTURED TEACHING

Chapter 1 Learning, or Not Learning, in School 1

Chapter 2 Focus Lessons: Establishing Purpose and
Modeling 17

Chapter 3 Guided Instruction: Cues, Prompts, and Questions 39

Chapter 4 Collaborative Learning: Consolidating
Thinking with Peers 62

Chapter 5 Independent Learning Tasks: Not Just
"Do It Yourself School". 86

Chapter 6 Implementing a Gradual Release of
Responsibility Model 110

References 134

Index 141

About the Authors 145

119420

1

Learning, or Not Learning, in School

Learning—the goal of schooling—is a complex process. But what is learning? It's a bit more complex than most people think. Consider the following definitions of learning and the implications each has for teaching:

- The process of acquiring knowledge or skill through study, experience, or teaching
- Experience that brings about a relatively permanent change in behavior
- A change in neural function as a consequence of experience
- The cognitive process of acquiring skills or knowledge
- An increase in the amount of response rules and concepts in the memory of an intelligent system

Which definition fits with your beliefs? How is it that you learn? Think of something that you do well. Take a minute to analyze this skill or behavior. How did you develop your prowess? How did you move from novice to expert?

We would argue that the things you do well were taught to you through a series of intentional actions. You probably did not develop high levels of skills from simply being told how to complete tasks. Instead, you likely had models, feedback, peer support, and lots of practice. Over time, you developed your expertise. You may even have learned more when you had to share that expertise with others. The model that explains this type of learning environment is called the *gradual release of responsibility*.

Gradual Release of Responsibility

The gradual release of responsibility model of instruction suggests that the cognitive load should shift slowly and purposefully from teacher-as-model, to joint responsibility, to independent practice and application by the learner (Pearson & Gallagher, 1983). The gradual release of responsibility model stipulates that the teacher moves from assuming "all the responsibility for performing a task . . . to a situation in which the students assume all of the responsibility" (Duke & Pearson, 2002, p. 211). This gradual release may occur over a day, a week, a month, or a year. Graves and Fitzgerald (2003) note "effective instruction often follows a progression in which teachers gradually do less of the work and students gradually assume increased responsibility for their learning. It is through this process of gradually assuming more and more responsibility for their learning that students become competent, independent learners" (p. 98).

The gradual release of responsibility model is the intersection of several theories, including the following:

- Piaget's (1952) work on cognitive structures and schema
- Vygotsky's (1962, 1978) work on zones of proximal development

2

- Bandura's (1965) work on attention, retention, reproduction, and motivation
- Wood, Bruner, and Ross's (1976) work on scaffolded instruction

Taken together, these theories suggest that learning occurs through interactions with others, and when these interactions are intentional, specific learning occurs. Unfortunately, most current implementation efforts of the gradual release of responsibility model limit these interactions to adult and child exchanges. A common framework for implementing the model is *I do it; we do it; you do it*. In other words, many current models lack a vital component: learning through collaboration with peers.

The effectiveness of peer learning has been demonstrated with English language learners (Gersten & Baker, 2000), students with disabilities (Stevens & Slavin, 1995), and learners identified as gifted (Coleman & Gallagher, 1995). While the effectiveness of peer learning has been documented, it has typically been examined as a singular practice, isolated from the overall instructional design of the lesson. A more complete implementation model for the gradual release of responsibility moves from modeled to guided instruction, followed by collaborative learning, and finally independent experiences (see Figure 1.1).

The four instructional arrangements contained within Figure 1.1 include focus lessons, guided instruction, collaborative learning, and independent tasks. Each of these will be explored in greater detail in subsequent chapters. At this point, we will provide an overview of each of these such that we can then discuss situations in which students aren't learning.

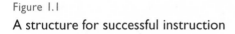

Figure 1.1

A structure for successful instruction

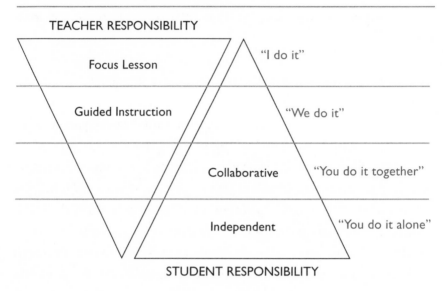

Focus Lessons

In the gradual release of responsibility model, the focus lesson is the modeling phase. For a focus lesson to be effective, teachers must clearly establish a purpose and model their own thinking. Consider, for example, the teacher who clearly communicates the purpose of the lesson as follows:

> Our content goal today is to multiply and estimate products of fractions and mixed numerals. Our language goal for today is to use mathematical terminology while discussing problems and answers with your peers. Our social goal today is to improve our turn-taking skills by making sure that each member of the group has a chance to participate in the discussion.

4

As Dick, Carey, and Carey (2001, p. 25) remind us, an "instructional goal is (1) a clear, general statement of learner outcomes, (2) related to an identified problem and needs assessment, and (3) achievable through instruction." These are three important considerations for establishing purpose. As we will discuss further in the chapter on focus lessons, it's not enough to simply state the purpose. We must ensure that students have opportunities to engage with the purpose and obtain feedback about their performance.

In addition to establishing purpose, the focus lesson should provide students with information about the ways in which a skilled reader, writer, or thinker processes information. Most often, this is done through a think-aloud (see Kucan & Beck, 1997) in which the teacher models the type of thinking required to solve problems, understand directions, comprehend a text, or the like. For example, after reading aloud a passage about spiders to 3rd graders, a teacher might say:

> Now I have even more questions. I wonder how spiders eat if they don't have mouth parts. I can't really visualize that, so I think I'll look for more information to answer my question. I do remember something very interesting. I didn't know that spiders are found all over the world. I think that the most interesting spider is the one that lives underwater in silken domes. Now that is something I need to know more about.

Focus lessons are almost always done with the whole class and typically last 15 minutes or less. The point is to clearly establish purpose and to ensure that students have a model from which to work.

Guided Instruction

Another phase of instruction occurs as teachers meet with needs-based groups. Guided instruction is almost always done with small, purposeful groups, which are composed based on students' performance on formative assessments. A number of instructional strategies can be used during guided instruction that will be explored further in a subsequent chapter. The key to guided instruction lies in the planning. These are not random groups of students meeting with the teacher. Instead, the groups consist of students who share a common instructional need that the teacher can address.

Guided instruction is an ideal time to differentiate. As Tomlinson (2001) has noted, teachers can differentiate content, process, and product. Small-group instruction allows teachers to vary the instructional materials they use, the level of prompting or questioning they employ, and the products they expect. For example, a 7th grade science teacher identified a group of five students who did not perform well on the pre-assessment questions related to the impacts of asteroids. He met with this group of students and shared with them a short book from the school library called *Comets, Asteroids, and Meteorites* (Gallant, 2000). He asked students to each read specific pages related to asteroids and then to have a discussion with him about the potential impact that these bodies might have on Earth. During this 20-minute lesson, the teacher validated and extended his students' understanding that the history of life on Earth has been disrupted by major catastrophic events, including asteroids. At one point in their discussion, the teacher asked the group of students:

> Consider what you know about the Earth's surface. Talk about that—is it all flat? [Students all respond no.] What do

you think are the things that made the surface of the Earth look like it does? The Earth has a history.

Of course, a single guided instructional event is not going to ensure that students suddenly develop the content knowledge or skills they were lacking. However, a series of guided instructional events will do so. Over time, and with cues, prompts, and questions, teachers can guide students to increasingly complex thinking. Guided instruction is, in part, about establishing high expectations and providing the support for students to reach those expectations.

Collaborative Learning

As we have noted, this phase of instruction is almost always neglected. If used, collaborative learning is often a special event and not an established instructional routine. The key to collaborative learning is the requirement for independent products from this group collaboration. This approach differs from many group-learning situations in which one product is produced. In those situations, teachers are often concerned that one student did all of the work while the others talked.

When collaborative learning is done right, our experience suggests that it is during this phase of instruction that students consolidate their thinking and understanding. Negotiating with peers, discussing ideas and information, or engaging in inquiry with others causes students to use what they learned during focus lessons and guided instruction. Importantly, collaborative learning is not the time to introduce new information to students. Rather, collaborative learning should be a time for students to apply information in novel situations or to engage in a spiral review of previous knowledge.

While meeting with small groups of students to facilitate their understanding of the historical importance of revolutions, a 10th grade social studies teacher has selected a number of readings that will allow students to compare and contrast the Glorious Revolution of England, the American Revolution, and the French Revolution. These students do so through reciprocal teaching (Oczkus, 2003; Palincsar & Brown, 1984) in which groups of four students read a piece of text in common and then discuss the text using predicting, questioning, summarizing, and clarifying. During the reciprocal teaching discussion, students take notes. At the end of the discussion, each student in this class is asked to summarize the reading individually. This individual accountability is key to the success of collaborative learning.

Listening in on one of the groups of students as they talk about their reading reveals the ways in which peers can support one another in the consolidation of information.

> *Jamal:* I still don't get it. Those folks in England had a revolution because the king wanted the army to be Catholic, and he got his own friends in government. But I need help to clarify what they mean by the "Dispensing Power." It sounds all Harry Potter.

> *Antone:* I feel you. But that's just the name for getting rid of rules you don't want.

> *LaSheika:* That king, James number 2, used a power he had to suspend laws and other rules. Adding that to the things you said already made people very angry, and they started the revolution to get rid of him. It's just like the other revolutions we talked about.

These collaborative learning situations help students think through key ideas, are a natural opportunity for inquiry, and ensure that students engage in content learning. As such, they are critical to the successful implementation of the gradual release of responsibility model of instruction.

Independent Tasks

The ultimate goal of our instruction is that students can independently apply information, ideas, content, skills, and strategies in unique situations. Our goal is not to create learners who are dependent on another person for information and ideas. As such, students need practice in completing independent tasks. To facilitate independent learning, the school and instructional events must be "organized to encourage and support a continued, increasingly mature and comprehensive acceptance of responsibilities for one's own learning" (Kesten, 1987, p. 15). Unfortunately, too many students are asked to complete independent tasks in the absence of good instruction that ensures that they have the background knowledge to do so. While there are a range of independent tasks that ensure students can apply information, our experience suggests that the more authentic the task is, the more likely the student is to complete it.

As with collaborative learning, students should not be asked to do unfamiliar tasks—tasks for which they have not had instruction—independently. Independent tasks should require individual application of information previously taught. These tasks should provide students with opportunities to use their knowledge to produce new products. For example, a kindergarten teacher might ask a student to read a familiar book to three adults, a 6th grade science teacher might ask a student to write a prediction of the outcome of a lab based on the previous three experiments, and a high school art teacher might ask a student to incorporate light and perspective into a new painting. These tasks are clearly related to the instruction each student received, yet each provides students an opportunity to apply that knowledge in a new way.

When Learning Isn't Occurring

Unfortunately, there are still classrooms in which responsibility is not being transferred from knowledgeable others (teachers, peers, parents) to students. These classrooms do not operate on an apprenticeship model in which scaffolding is used to ensure success. For example, in some classrooms, teachers provide modeling and then ask students to complete independent tasks. This approach is graphically represented in Figure 1.2.

Figure 1.2
In some classrooms . . .

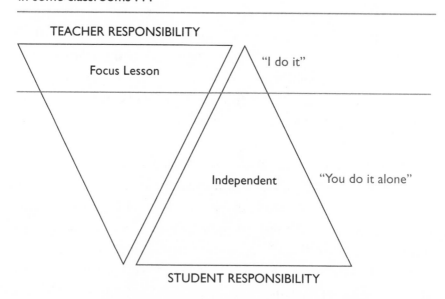

This instructional model is all too familiar. The teacher demonstrates how to solve algebra problems and then asks students to solve the odd-numbered problems in the back of the book. Or a teacher reads a text aloud and then asks students to complete a comprehension worksheet based on the reading. In both of these cases, the teacher fails to develop students' understanding of the content through purposeful interactions.

Sadly, there is a classroom model worse than this, at least in terms of instructional development. In some classrooms, students are asked to learn independently day after day. This approach is graphically represented in Figure 1.3.

Figure 1.3
In some classrooms . . .

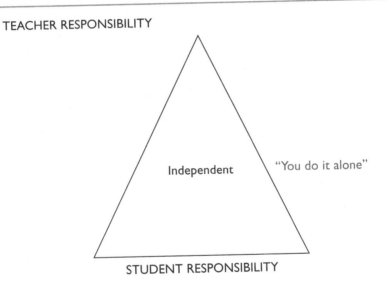

TEACHER RESPONSIBILITY

Independent   "You do it alone"

STUDENT RESPONSIBILITY

Some teachers assign pages from a textbook to be read and then require students to answer questions at the back of the book, over and over again. Other teachers spend hours at the photocopy machine creating packets for students to work on independently, hour after hour. There really isn't much teaching going on in these classrooms. It's mostly assigning or causing work.

Frankly, we'd be embarrassed to cash our paychecks if we taught like this. However, we want to be careful in the discussion about independent work. There are days at school where students need to spend significant amounts of time completing projects, writing essays, and the like. However, this type of work does not occur every day, and it is based on the instruction that occurs in focus lessons, guided instruction, and collaborative learning.

But even in classrooms that most people would consider "good" or "good enough," the gradual release of responsibility model is not fully operationalized. Commonly, the collaborative learning phase is missing. This approach is graphically represented in Figure 1.4.

Figure 1.4

And in some classrooms . . .

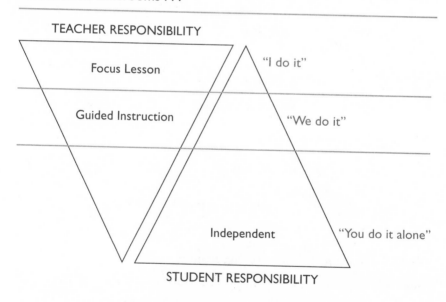

In these classrooms, the teacher models and then meets with small groups of students. Unfortunately, students don't have an opportunity to collaborate, as they are all required to complete independent tasks while waiting their turn to meet with the teacher. For example, the teacher might model comprehension strategies useful in understanding scientific texts and then meet with two or three small groups of students to guide their understanding. While this happens, the rest of the students need to be in collaborative-learning groups. Unfortunately, they are more likely to be assigned independent reading from a textbook instead.

We believe that all four components are necessary for students to learn. Neglecting one or more of the stages in this progression will not result in deep learning, critical or creative thinking, or the ability to mobilize strategies as needed. Instead, we will have reinforced students who attempt to memorize facts for tests and not students who become independent, lifelong learners. But we didn't always understand this need to include all four components. Our teaching histories are replete with all of the examples described earlier.

When the Importance of Gradual Release Became Real for Us

The gradual release of responsibility model has been around for decades. We have used it in our preservice classes as well as in our teaching of public school students. But the day we fully understood the importance of this model was January 16. We were in Las Vegas, Nevada, at a conference. We were staying at the Venetian hotel, a very nice place to stay. Doug had a cell phone on his hip, the old kind of cell phone that did one thing only—it made phone calls. It did not take pictures, send e-mail, or do anything else fancy.

While Doug was walking through the lobby, his phone rang. As he tried to answer it, it fell from his hip into the lagoon. Down the drain it went. Given that Doug couldn't imagine a weekend without a cell phone, we took a taxi to the local Sprint store to obtain a new phone. Doug wanted to exercise his insurance policy and get a free replacement phone.

The salesman saw it differently. He wanted to make a new sale, so he redirected Doug from the "old school" phones to ones that were high-tech. As the salesman said, "You need a phone that is more intuitive, one that has e-mail, an address book, a calendar program, and can search the Web." Doug assured him that no, he did not need any of these things. The salesman was very persistent and noted that the newer phones sent text messages. Doug had never sent a text message in his life, nor had the need ever arisen. But the salesman was skilled. He said, "You know, the young people all send text messages. It's the new way of communicating." Doug wants to be a young person, so out came his credit card, and he bought the new Treo 650. Doug was very proud of his new, high-tech purchase. The salesman took the phone out of the box and demonstrated all kinds of features.

About an hour later, back at the hotel, the phone rang. There it sat, buzzing away, but Doug did not know how to answer it. There wasn't anything to flip open, like the old phone, and there wasn't any obvious button that said "answer." Frustrated, we got back in the taxi and returned to the Sprint store.

Of course, Doug couldn't bear to tell the salesman that he couldn't work the phone. Instead, Doug handed the phone to him and said, "I think it's broken." The salesman—we'll call him Steve—immediately took the phone out of Doug's hands and started working the phone. Standing in the store, Doug suddenly felt very guilty and turned to Nancy and said, "How many times have I modeled comprehension for students only to take away the task and do it for them when they had difficulty?" Clearly this approach is a violation of the gradual release of responsibility model. What learners need when they experience difficulty is guided instruction, not more modeling. Frustrated learners already know that their teacher can complete the task; the teacher has demonstrated it several times. What the frustrated learner needs is guided practice, with the scaffolding there to ensure success.

Anyway, back to the store. Doug turned to Steve and said, "I really don't need another focus lesson; I need some guided instruction. Can I hold the phone while you talk me through the operation?" Steve was a little puzzled, but he complied. He guided, prompted, questioned, and cued Doug on how to use the phone. Nancy got so caught up in the experience that she decided, on the spot, to buy a new Treo 650 as well.

Of course the combination of the focus lesson and one guided instructional event did not ensure that we could use our new technology independently. What we needed was the opportunity to practice, without the teacher (or, in this case, the salesman) providing cues. As Doug said to Nancy, "I'm too embarrassed to ask him how to do it again. We'll have to figure it out." Well, figure it out, slowly and over time, we did. That night, at dinner at the Capitol Grill, we sat across the table from each other sending text messages. We collaborated, problem solving as we went.

Over several weeks, with much practice and peer support, we both incorporated this new technology into our lives. In thinking about this experience, we realized that everything we each know how to do well, we learned through this process of modeling, guided practice, collaborative learning, and independent application. We also realized that the things we don't do well were simply told to us, without the opportunity to engage with scaffolds and supports for learning. On that day, the importance of the gradual release of responsibility model of instruction became real.

Conclusion

We have presented the gradual release of responsibility as an instructional model that ensures better student learning through structured teaching. This instructional model is intentional, purposeful, and explicit. However, we want to distinguish this approach from highly prescriptive teaching. Gradual Release of Responsibility is not a script that teachers follow. Instead, this model helps teachers increase precision in their teaching. As Fullan, Hill, and Crévola (2006) note, we don't need more prescriptive teaching, but rather more precision in our teaching. Precision teaching requires that teachers know their students and content well, that they regularly assess students' understanding of the content, and that they purposefully plan lessons that transfer responsibility from the teacher to the student. It is through this very purposeful classroom structure that learning occurs.

CHAPTER 2

Focus Lessons: Establishing Purpose and Modeling

The first phase of a gradual release of responsibility model is the focus lesson. This is the time when the teacher is demonstrating, modeling, and sharing his or her thinking with students. Although this segment may be brief (5–15 minutes), it is powerful. This is the time when the teacher uses the students' attention to introduce the concept, skill, or strategy they are to learn. This task is accomplished through one or more approaches designed to make the learning transparent to learners. The notion of transparency is critical to the focus lesson. In order for students to acquire new knowledge, they need to witness a more knowledgeable other (the teacher) using the strategy being demonstrated. Moreover, they need to be invited into the mind of that more knowledgeable other. This is accomplished by sharing one's thinking—making it transparent to students not only how it is done but how decisions are made in the successful completion of the task.

What Focus Lessons Are Not

Focus lessons are not intended as a time to ask students questions. During the focus lesson, the teacher should model his or her thinking and not interrogate students about their thinking. As such, the teacher should use a number of "I" statements, such as "I think . . ." or "I wonder . . ." or "I predict . . . ." The teacher should not turn the table during this phase of instruction and, after reading a passage aloud, ask students about their predictions, questions, inferences, or the like. Of course, the teacher can ask students to talk with a partner to practice the skill or strategy of the focus lesson following the teacher modeling. The important thing to remember is that students need modeling— examples—that they can incorporate into their habits.

Far too many students have been questioned about things they don't understand and have not been provided with the examples they need to be successful. As teachers, we commonly ask students questions for which we already have the answers. Students call this approach "Guess what's in the teacher's brain"; researchers call it initiate, respond, evaluate (I-R-E) (Cazden, 1988). A typical sequence of instruction, in the absence of teacher modeling, might go something like this:

Teacher: Why did Lewis and Clark want to explore the west? (Initiate)

Student 1: To discover California? (Respond)

Teacher: Well, not really. (Evaluate) What do others think? (Initiate)

Student 2: To get some gold? (Respond)

Teacher: No, not yet. (Evaluate) Before the Gold Rush, why did Lewis and Clark want to explore? (Initiate)

Clearly, the students do not know the answer that the teacher is looking for. Using a gradual release of responsibility model, the teacher would have first modeled his or her thinking, probably from a piece of text. Consider the difference when the teacher does so. In this case, the teacher reads aloud a portion of the letter President Thomas Jefferson wrote on June 20, 1803, to Meriwether Lewis:

> The Object of your mission is to explore the Missouri river & such principal stream of it as by it's course and communication with the waters of the Pacific ocean, whether the Columbia, Oregon, Colorado or any other river may offer the most direct & practicable water communication across this continent for the purpose of commerce. (Lewis, Bergon, & Clark, 2003, p. xxiv)

During and after the reading of this passage, the teacher thinks aloud, sharing her understanding of the text. Along the way, she notes that the president of the United States is interested in a water route across the United States. She also notes that his purpose in forming the expedition is for commerce, or conducting business. In doing so, she facilitates her students' thinking about not only the reasons for the expedition but also how to read for information.

Focus lessons are also not the time to simply tell students things. The key to a quality focus lesson is *explaining*. As we will discuss later in this chapter, students need an explanation of their teachers' cognitive and metacognitive processes. As we discussed in Chapter 1, people don't really learn from being told. Learners need scaffolds and supports to process information. This need has implications for every classroom. As teachers, we should continually ask ourselves whether we are explaining or telling.

This question has profound implications for lectures in middle and high school. A good lecture lets the participants in on the thinking and does not simply regurgitate information that could have been read. What students do not need is an "information dump" from teacher to student. A good lecture should model critical thinking for students as the "teacher questions her own assumptions, acknowledges ethical dilemmas hidden in her position, refers to inconvenient theories, facts, and philosophies that she has deliberately overlooked, and demonstrates an openness to alternative viewpoints" (Brookfield, 1995, p. 19). The worthwhile lecture, though brief in nature, should convey new terms and concepts and draw connections between ideas as the lecturer explains the thinking behind the information.

In addition, the focus lesson is not a time in which students read aloud to the rest of the class. Although there are instructional reasons for students reading aloud, such as choral reading or for diagnostics, the focus lesson is not one of these times. As we like to say, the focus lesson is the time in which the person who is paid to be there reads or thinks aloud. Evidence indicates that asking students to read unfamiliar texts aloud to the whole class is harmful to the individual student and counterproductive for the rest of the class, as they are often hearing a disfluent reading (Opitz & Rasinski, 1998). The comedian Lily Tomlin still talks about an experience she had in 2nd grade. While reading aloud to the whole class, she mispronounced *island*. From that point on, she was teased at school and began to dislike not only school but also herself. It's pretty powerful when an experience from 2nd grade is still on your mind when you're in your 60s. What students need is for a fluent reader to read, explain, and share the thinking required of the text or the task (Duffy, 2003).

Key Features of Focus Lessons

Before we provide examples of strategies for developing and delivering focus lessons, let's explore two key features. First, all focus lessons should establish a purpose for the learning. Marzano, Pickering, and Pollock (2001) note that establishing purpose— setting objectives and providing feedback, as they call it—is one of the classroom instructional strategies that matters. Similarly, Hill and Flynn (2006) suggest that establishing purpose is critical to the success of English language learners. As they note, too many students don't know what to pay attention to or what really matters. As a result, students fail to learn the content they are exposed to.

Teachers establish purpose in a variety of ways. Unfortunately, in many districts, this good idea has been misapplied and minimized to a requirement for posting the standards on the wall. Simply posting standards on the wall is not establishing purpose with students. Students need to be involved in the process, to talk about the purpose, and to understand the goal of the instruction. Students need to be provided with clear explanations of the purpose and the activities that are linked with the purpose.

The types of purpose that are established also vary. As we noted in Chapter 1, teachers can establish purpose in three domains: content, language, and social. The example in Chapter 1 was from a mathematics classroom. Consider the following example from a science classroom. The teacher establishes purpose immediately following the writing prompt that students responded to upon entering the classroom. The prompt for this 4th grade classroom read, "When a little kid asks me about a food chain, I will explain it like this . . . ." The teacher says:

> As you know or could predict from our writing prompt, we're
> still focused on the food chain. Today, we're going to focus on

the primary source of matter and energy in the food chain— plants. We need to learn more about plants as a source of matter and energy. In doing so, I want to be sure that we're paying attention to our key terms: producers, and consumers such as herbivores, carnivores, omnivores, and decompos- ers. I also want to make sure that we remember to write in complete sentences, not fragments. And, finally, our social goal for the week is to actively listen while others are speak- ing. To accomplish these things, I'll be reading and talking about plants with you, and then you'll be reading, talking, and writing. Some of you will be on computers doing Inter- net research; others will be reading more about decompos- ers such as fungi, insects, and microorganisms that recycle matter from dead plants and animals; and others will watch a short film about this.

Establishing the purpose is a critical component of the focus lesson. The other key feature is modeling thinking. As the exam- ple of the 4th grade teacher here suggests, one of the ways to meet the purpose is for the teacher to model his or her thinking for students. Again, modeling thinking should be brief and should result in students' incorporating strategies into their habits. As we noted in the previous section, the focus is on *explaining* and not telling. In the next section, we'll dive deeply into modeling.

Instructional Strategies for Effective Focus Lessons

The three methods used most often in the focus lesson phase are *modeling, metacognitive awareness,* and *think-alouds.* Although closely related, these three techniques serve different purposes. Modeling emphasizes cognition—that is, how a skill, task, or strategy is accomplished. Metacognition extends the cognition through monitoring the use of the content being learned. The final approach, think-alouds, combines cognition and metacognition as the teacher shares how he or she uses both to understand the content. Think-alouds showcase sophisticated levels of knowing because the process gives learners a window into the mind of an expert. Together these represent a gradual release of responsibility across a series of focus lessons.

Modeling

The focus lesson is first and foremost an opportunity to model a task or skill. However, as noted before, modeling can easily devolve into telling rather than teaching. Modeling is different because it follows a precise pattern:

1. *Name the strategy, skill, or task.* "Today I am going to show you how to combine sentences to make more interesting and complex statements."

2. *State the purpose of the strategy, skill, or task.* "It's important as a writer to be able to construct sentences that aren't repetitive or choppy. Sentence combining is one way to make sure your sentences read more smoothly."

3. *Explain when the strategy or skill is used.* "After I have written a passage, I reread it to see if I have choppy sentences or if I am repeating information unnecessarily. When I notice that's occurred, I look for ways to combine sentences."

4. *Use analogies to link prior knowledge to new learning.* "I like to think of this as making sure I make a straight path for my reader to follow. When I eliminate choppy or redundant sentences, it's like making a straight path of ideas for them to follow."

5. *Demonstrate how the skill, strategy, or task is completed.* "I'm going to show you three short, choppy sentences. Let's look first at information that we can cross out because it is repetitive.

Then I'm going to combine those three sentences into one longer and more interesting sentence."

6. *Alert learners about errors to avoid.* "I have to be careful not to cut out too much information, so that I don't lose the meaning. I also need to watch out for sentences that become too long. A reader can lose the meaning of a sentence that's too long."

7. *Access the use of the skill.* "Now I'm going to reread my new sentence to see if it makes sense."

When learners have a skill or strategy modeled, and not just merely told, they gain a deeper understanding for when to apply it, what to watch out for, and how to analyze their success. This is consistent with four dimensions of learning: declarative (*What is it?*), procedural (*How do I use it?*), conditional (*When and where do I use it?*), and reflective (*How do I know I used it correctly?*) (Angelo, 1991). You can also see elements of metacognition emerging in the modeling lesson. Students are not just being taught how to do something; they are being primed to analyze the success of their use of what they are learning.

Direct Explanation. This modeling technique requires the teacher to state explicitly what a process is and how it is to be used, including a model of how it looks or sounds (Duffy, Roehler, & Rackliffe, 1986). This is accompanied by a clear sequence of instructions that feature consistent use of language and precise terminology. For example, in her geometry class, Ms. Nguyen established the purpose of the lesson, which centered on measuring exterior angles of triangles. She also explained her language goal (to incorporate vocabulary into discussions and proofs) and social goals (to collaborate with peers in a group project). Before asking students to work in groups and solve problems and proofs, she provided a direct explanation of her thinking. She read the definition of the theorem: "The measure of an exterior angle of a triangle is equal to the sum of the measures of the two non-adjacent interior angles." She then explained her understanding of the theorem:

> I know that "sum" is to add up. It's the answer when we add something up. I also know that "nonadjacent" means "not next to." *Non* means "not," and *adjacent* means "next to or near." So, this theorem is saying to me that the measure of the exterior angle—this one [she points to an exterior angle]—is equal to the sum of the two that are not directly next to the exterior angle I'm trying to figure out. I also know that some people call the nonadjacent angles remote interior angles, but that doesn't really help me here.

She then looks at a problem: "In $\triangle PQR$, $m\angle Q = 45°$, and $m\angle R = 72°$. Find the measure of an exterior angle at P." Again, she shares her thinking through direct explanation.

> Okay, so I know that one angle is 45° and the other one is 72°. Wait, I don't have to do this in my head. It is always helpful to draw a diagram and label it with the given information. Let's see, I'll label the triangle like this and see if it helps. Yes, it does. Now I can see which are nonadjacent angles and which I need to solve. Easy, now it's just a calculation problem. I'm ready for another.

She continues this way through two more examples and then moves into guided instruction, first with the whole class and then with small groups. While she does so, she provides students in their collaborative learning groups proofs to work on and reminds them to use the academic vocabulary they have learned in their discussions and on the proof pages.

Demonstration. Think of the times you have tuned in to a television show to watch a demonstration of a complicated process you were interested in learning. It may have been a show on making a soufflé, or redecorating a living room, or casting a fly fishing rod, but in all cases it was accompanied by the narration of an expert who explained what he or she was doing. The combination of verbal and visual elements reinforced the most salient features of the task.

Ms. Lattner has begun a watercolor painting unit in her middle school art class. Her students need to learn how to stretch the paper correctly in order to have a satisfactory result with their final product. She begins by naming all the materials she will need for the task, including watercolor paper, art tape, clean water and two sponges, and a board for mounting the paper.

> The first thing I need to do is check to make sure I have the side of the paper I want to use facing up. I can paint on either side, but I like to use the rougher side of the paper because it seems to hold my paint better. I can run my hand over both sides of the paper to figure out which side is rougher. The paper needs to soak in the water for a few minutes, so I am going to place it in the pan and set the timer for three minutes. That way I won't forget. I used tepid water, which means water that is around room temperature, in the pan. Hot water can ruin the paper. While it is soaking, I'll cut the strips of tape I'll need to mount the paper on the board. I have to make sure that the tape isn't shorter than the length of each side. If it is, the paper will dry funny, and I'll have a big bubble in it.

After the timer rings, Ms. Lattner continues.

I'm going to be careful as I lift the paper because I want as much water as possible to drain off it. I can't put a sopping wet paper on the board, or it will take forever for it to dry.

She holds the paper above the pan to allow the excess water to drain.

I think that's as much water as I'm going to get off of the paper that way. I've been watching the amount of water dripping in the pan, and it has slowed down to almost nothing. I know I can get water off another way. I'm going to lay the paper down on the board and use this sponge to smooth it. I've checked the sponge to make sure it's clean, and now I'm going to smooth it using long strokes across the paper. The sponge absorbs water as it smooths. Now that the paper is smooth, I need to tape it down. This tape gets sticky on one side, but only after it gets wet. I use a brown sponge for wetting the tape, so that I never mix up my smoothing sponges with my taping ones. You know why? Because that sticky stuff from the tape gets on the sponge. If I accidentally use that sponge later for smoothing, I'll get it all over the paper, and it will be ruined.

The teacher places the tape on all four edges of the paper and affixes it to the wooden board.

Now it's done! It needs to dry overnight, and when I check it tomorrow, it will be very tight and smooth. As the paper dries, it contracts, which means it gets a bit smaller. The tape holds it in place, so the contraction of the paper stretches it tight. When I paint on it, the surface will be smooth, and it won't crinkle up as I apply the watercolors to it.

This demonstration included not only the sequence of steps but also insights into how decisions are made about when to go on to the next step. In addition, Ms. Lattner carefully noted the errors to avoid when completing this task.

Teaching for Metacognitive Awareness

A second aspect of a successful focus lesson is teaching for metacognitive awareness. This is defined as the learner's mindful acknowledgment of his or her own learning processes, the conditions under which he or she learns best, and a recognition that learning has occurred. Metacognitive awareness is truly a lifelong phenomenon and is therefore not taught in a handful of lessons. Instead, it is something that teachers must return to again and again. This is accomplished through focus lessons that provide students with time to recognize that learning has occurred and under what conditions. Therefore, focus lessons with a metacognitive component ask students to analyze how they are applying a strategy.

Anderson (2002) has developed a series of four questions that challenge learners to move from cognition to metacognition. We will expand on each of these questions. We post these questions on the board at the beginning of a focus lesson and write the answers as we move through the lesson.

1. *"What am I trying to accomplish?"* This first question moves the learners from merely copying a task to analyzing the outcomes. We've long heard the reminder to "begin with the end in mind" (Covey, 2004, p. 65). Therefore, we pose this question and answer it for our students. "This math word problem is asking me to figure out how many people can be served with the number of apple pies at the picnic."

2. *"What strategies am I using?"* After identifying the problem and the goal, the next step is to figure out what strategies can be used to achieve a solution. "I really need to use two strategies to find the answer. First, I have to multiply the number of slices by the total number of pies. That will give me the total number of servings. But then I also have to divide those servings among the people at the picnic."

3. *"How well am I using the strategies?"* Once again, monitoring plays an important role in the acquisition of new learning. The answer to this question shows students that control of a skill or strategy comes from pausing from time to time during the process to see whether it's working. "Before I divide, I need to check to see if what I've multiplied makes sense. Could it be that 8 apple pies could be cut into a total of 64 slices? I also want to check my math. Does 8 times 8 equal 64?"

4. *"What else could I do?"* The goal of this question is to teach students to think flexibly, rather than allow themselves to be bogged down in the rigid thinking that often comes with a new skill. It is common at this stage of learning for students to temporarily forget that they have learned other skills or strategies previously. Remind them that those familiar strategies have a role. "I'm still not sure I am doing this correctly. One way I can be sure is if I draw a diagram of the pies and the people. We've done that before when we've had tough word problems. I'm going to try that now."

Notice how the metacognitive awareness focus lesson differs from modeling and how it represents a gradual release of responsibility within this phase of instruction. In the metacognition focus lesson, the emphasis shifts to direct instruction on a framework for making decisions about the use of the skill or strategy. Students have already had a focus lesson or two on how to perform these operations. They are now ready to see how to examine ways to prepare and plan, select an approach, and monitor the execution of their plan (Anderson, 2002). The teacher has shifted away from the step-by-step instruction during the modeling phase; there is less attention on direct explanation and demonstration.

Public Problem Solving. Novices have difficulty bridging the "how" of new learning to the "where" and "when" of using the skill or strategy. Public problem solving is a demonstration of the metacognitive processes an expert engages in, as the teacher makes his or her thinking transparent to learners.

Ms. Dykstra's 1st grade students have been reading a passage in their social studies textbooks about representative and direct democracies. She knows this is a challenging concept for 7-year-olds and wants to use this opportunity to show how she untangles this confusion.

> When I was reading that last section, I got those two ideas all jumbled up in my head. I thought I understood, but when I tried to restate it in my head, I realized I didn't have it yet. So I looked back in the book to help myself. The first thing I did was look for the bolded words. I remember there were bolded words and that there was a definition in the same sentence. I reread that to myself, and this time I did it as a whisper-read so I could hear myself.

She quietly reads the sentences aloud.

> That helped, I think. I am going to check myself to be sure. I'll close my book and see if I can say it in my own words. "A direct democracy means everyone gets to vote. A representative democracy means people choose someone to do the

voting for them." Now I'm going to check my answer with the book to see if I am right.

Ms. Dykstra shows her students throughout the day how she evaluates her own learning through monitoring and checking. She also reinforces strategies she has taught them previously by showing them when she applies them, such as rereading, finding bolded words, and reading aloud to herself when she runs into difficult text.

Think-alouds. Application is the end goal of a series of focus lessons, as focus lessons prepare learners for assuming more of the cognitive load needed in guided, collaborative, and independent learning. A think-aloud process provides the chance for the teacher to combine the cognition introduced through modeling with the thinking skills introduced through the metacognitive awareness lessons. The key to an effective think-aloud is that the teacher is using the first person to describe how he or she makes decisions, implements skills, activates problem-solving protocols, and evaluates whether success has been achieved. Importantly, this is a chance for students to witness how an expert merges declarative, procedural, conditional, and reflective knowledge in a fluent fashion. Fisher and Frey (2007b) describe five key considerations in crafting an effective think-aloud:

- *Keep the focus of the think-aloud tight and brief.* It is easy to get carried away with a think-aloud, allowing it to turn into a rambling monologue of every thought that wanders through your head. Choose a short piece of written text, a single math word problem, or one example of a process. It is better to deliver a short but effective think-aloud than one that serves only to confuse the learner with too many details.

- *Pay attention to your own thinking processes as you design your think-aloud.* This is really very difficult when you are an expert at something. Nathan and Petrosino (2003) state that "well-developed subject matter knowledge can lead people to assume that learning should follow the structure of the subject-matter domain rather than the learning needs and developmental profiles of novices"—a phenomenon they call the "expert blind spot" (p. 906). In other words, when you've been very adept at something for a long time, it can be difficult to retrace your own learning footsteps to recall a time when this information was new to you. A successful think-aloud requires you to unpack your own thinking processes to understand how you arrive at understanding.

- *Find your authentic voice when you think aloud.* This approach requires lots of "I" statements, which can feel contrived when you first begin. As teachers, it seems more comfortable to tell students, using lots of "you" statements. The problem with those statements is that our instruction reverts to direct explanation, rather than making the thinking of an expert transparent. It is useful to find an informal style and to resist adopting an overly academic voice. Your students will find it more helpful to hear you say, "Wow—when I first looked at this diagram of the solar system, I thought right away about what it didn't have in the illustration, like the asteroid belt and the dwarf planets," rather than, "I analyzed the diagram for the visual information it contained and immediately noted the small solar system bodies it did not contain."

- *Think like the expert you are.* Keeping a think-aloud authentic doesn't mean you have to check your expertise at the door. As a content area expert, you have the ability to share unique insights with your students. Effective think-alouds give you the opportunity to think like a mathematician, a scientist, an artist, a historian, an athlete, or a literary critic in front of your students.

• *Name your cognitive and metacognitive processes.* Labeling is critical if students are to build their own metacognitive awareness. Tell them when you are using the associative property of multiplication or making a text-to-text connection for reading comprehension—these are cognitive approaches you are teaching your students to use. In addition, signal your metacognition as you problem solve ("That didn't work, so I have to try a different formula"), acquire new knowledge ("That's something I didn't know until I read this article"), and regulate your learning ("I know that I usually understand an editorial better when I know who's written it, so I always look at the writer's affiliation first").

Keep in mind that the goal of a think-aloud is to let novices in on how an expert synthesizes skills and habits of mind.

Shared Reading. Holdaway (1979) pioneered this instructional approach as a way to bring the positive effects of story reading at home into the primary classroom. It has evolved into a practice that allows teachers to model how they apply reading comprehension strategies to text. In the past decade it has become a staple of secondary content classrooms as teachers use the dense informational readings of the course to show students how they understand the content. A key feature of a shared reading is the students' access to the text. Most commonly, the reading is projected on an overhead projector or with a document camera so that students can follow along as the teacher reads. Many teachers like to give students their own paper copy of the reading as well. Notice who is bearing the cognitive load—it is the teacher who is doing the reading, while students follow along silently. The teacher pauses throughout the reading to think aloud about the information and to explain his or her own mental processes in understanding the text.

Tenth grade biology teacher Mr. Brownlee has been teaching a unit about human immune response, and his students have been struggling with understanding the role of phagocytes in fighting disease. He reads, "Phagocytes destroy any foreign body, including the debris and dead cells produced by injury. It overwhelms the injured areas and engulfs the foreign bodies through a process called phagocytosis." Mr. Brownlee knows this statement contains a number of concepts that are easily misunderstood, so he pauses to think aloud:

> When I first learned about phagocytes, I couldn't really get my head around what they did. Then my biology professor told me that *phagocyte* means "a cell that eats." That helped me understand a bit more. A phagocyte doesn't eat like we do, but it swallows up the garbage that shouldn't be there. There's a word in that sentence that confirms my recollection of that idea. The word *engulf* means "to swallow something up, to surround it." Now I can connect that to one more idea in that sentence—phagocytosis. Anytime I see a word that ends in *-osis,* it's a signal to me that it is a process. So phagocytosis is the process used by a phagocyte, a cell that eats, to swallow up anything it thinks shouldn't belong there. I had to take that sentence apart to understand it, and I did it by analyzing the derivations of a science term, then confirming my understanding using other terms in the sentence.

Mr. Brownlee combines both cognition and metacognition to show his students how he understands this informational text as a biologist. He is also explicit in naming the strategies he activated so as not to leave it to chance whether his students would notice (or not).

Write-alouds. Another instructional approach we use often in our classrooms is writing aloud in front of students. It is said that writing is the most complex of the elements of literacy (reading, writing, speaking, listening, and viewing) because it is built upon all of the others. After all, writing represents ideas that are formulated through oral exchanges and listening to others as well as reading. The writer must command all of these processes with a measure of fluency in order to get it on the paper. In our view, writing aloud, which entails thinking aloud as one writes, is essential for improving writing among students.

The students in Ms. Ramachandran's 3rd grade classroom have been doing an author study of the works of Beverly Cleary. Groups of students have worked in literature circles (Daniels, 2001) that have collectively selected books by this prolific author. Students will select one of the titles and will compose a review for submission to the www.amazon.com Web site for others to see. Ms. Ramachandran knows that this complex task requires lots of instruction, and she has already done focus lessons on the elements of a good book review and the considerations for a good submission to the Web site, such as length and tone. She is now composing in front of her students, writing aloud as she develops a review of *A Girl from Yamhill* (Cleary, 1996), the book she read as part of the author study.

> My book was an autobiography of part of Beverly Cleary's life, and she wrote about her childhood and how she started writing her first book. It's going to be important to say that in my review, so that customers will know what it is about. Wait, I should write down some of these ideas so that I don't forget. That's brainstorming, when you make a list of ideas. I am going to write "autobiography" and "childhood" on my

list. I am also going to add "writes her first book." [She writes a list on chart paper.]

After brainstorming and noting ideas on her list, Ms. Rama-chandran begins to compose.

I'm going to start my review with a sentence about what the book is about, so that the customers will know just a bit about it. "*A Girl from Yamhill* is an autobiography by . . ."—wait, I'm changing that—"written by Beverly Cleary about her child-hood in Oregon."

As she speaks, the teacher writes the words on the chart paper.

I'm checking my brainstorming list to see if there is anything else I want to add. Yes, I wanted to put this in about how she wrote her first book. "The author also tells . . . "—I have a bet-ter word than that—"describes the time when she wrote her very first book." Now I need to reread what I've written so far to see if it makes sense.

She reads her first two sentences aloud and continues writing.

I wrote, "*A Girl from Yamhill* is an autobiography written by Beverly Cleary about her childhood in Oregon. The author also describes the time when she wrote her very first book." I'm checking for capitalization and punctuation, and it looks like I've done everything correctly. Now I have to add some sentences about my opinion of this book, because that's the purpose of a book review. Then I'll finish with recommendations.

This teacher's write-aloud captures the dynamics of writing. Many novices falsely believe that writing is a continuous laying down of sentences, word by word. Writing aloud in front of her students lets them witness the thinking processes used by a writer, including the editing she engages in from nearly the beginning of her piece.

Formative Assessments in Focus Lessons

Every phase of instruction must be accompanied by a means of checking for understanding, beginning with the focus lesson. This is most commonly done through oral and written summaries. With younger children, we usually have them "turn to a partner" to restate or summarize what they have just learned. We listen in to conversations and make notes on a transparency of what we have overheard. These notes are projected onto the screen, and we discuss the accuracy and completeness of the conversations ("Anthony and Tre: Our classroom is a direct democracy because everyone has a vote, but our student council is a representative democracy because we elect leaders to vote for us"). This is an excellent way to find out what they understood—and misunderstood—which provides direction for the next lesson.

Several social and language goals are achieved at the same time. Partner talk allows us to promote social relationships among students and is particularly useful for English language learners who may be reluctant to participate in whole-class discussions. At the same time, it provides novices with an opportunity to use the academic language of the content in their retelling. An example of this is when Ms. Nguyen, the geometry teacher, checked for understanding and told students the terminology they needed to use in their explanation. Finally, this procedure gives us a chance to build community in the classroom. We will often share the thinking of some of the quieter members of the class to build their social capital. Older students don't always appreciate the attention, so we usually place their comments anonymously. They enjoy the recognition privately, while we still get to put good ideas out there in the class for everyone to consider.

This process works equally well in writing. A "ticket out the door" (Fisher & Frey, 2007b) is written during the last few minutes of the class period and handed to the teacher on the way out of the classroom. The teacher can quickly skim through the summaries to determine what, if anything, needs to be retaught the following day. This can also be done using other writing forms, including drawings and diagrams. Ms. Lattner asked her students to illustrate the steps of stretching watercolor paper; then she returned these illustrations the following day so they could refer to their directions as they performed the task.

Conclusion

There are many ways to establish purpose, model thinking, demonstrate skills, and teach for metacognition; we have listed only a few. Recall that the essential features of focus lessons include modeling and direct explanation of the skills, strategies, or tasks being taught. This is followed by teacher-led metacognitive awareness lessons that show students when and how to use new learning, as well as how to evaluate the success of the approach they have selected. Finally, these cognitive and metacognitive processes are merged through think-alouds, time when the teacher is demonstrating how both are used in a fluent and coherent manner.

3

Guided Instruction: Cues, Prompts, and Questions

The guided instruction phase of the gradual release of responsibility framework is the time when the cognitive load begins to shift from teacher to student. Until now, the teacher has carried the responsibility for knowing, leading learners through modeling, and demonstrating the metacognitive awareness one needs to acquire in order to evaluate one's success. In guided instruction, the teacher's role changes as he or she follows the lead of the learner, who is attempting to apply the skill or strategy to a new situation. Margaret Mooney (1988) elegantly describes this change in the teacher's role as "to/for, with, and by," meaning that the teacher begins by modeling *to* or *for* learners, then works *with* them as a guide, and eventually is *by* their side as they become more independent. It's not unlike teaching a child to ride a bicycle—there's that critical window when you are running alongside the novice, reaching out to steady her when she begins to wobble, then releasing the seat once again when she has regained control. Knowing when to offer a steadying hand, and when to withdraw it, is truly the art and science of teaching.

Of course, you can't offer this level of precision teaching to an entire classroom at once. Guided instruction necessitates the use of small groups. This is time during the day when three to six students meet for teacher-guided instruction. The guiding occurs through cueing, prompting, scaffolding, and questioning. Meanwhile, the other students are engaged in collaborative learning (more on that topic in the next chapter). This guided instruction time is so valuable because it's your opportunity as a teacher to explore just what each student knows and doesn't know at that moment in time.

What Guided Instruction Is Not

Guided instruction is not ability grouping. Ability grouping, a permanent structure in which specific students are grouped with peers based on ability, is an ineffective way of increasing student performance and likely harms students' self-esteem (Flood, Lapp, Flood, & Nagel, 1992). Guided instruction is also not prescriptive, meaning that there isn't a script to follow for each guided lesson. So much depends on what the student says and does. The teacher needs a heightened sense of awareness at this time in order to make the next instructional move.

The teacher might ask himself or herself a series of questions, such as these: "Does this student need a bit of reteaching before he is able to explain the differences between meiosis and mitosis?" "Is this group ready to analyze a political cartoon critical of FDR's first hundred days in office, because they understand the controversies of the time regarding government interference?" "Do I expect some students to have difficulty recognizing a scalene triangle when it is shown in a different orientation?" This illustrative series of questions relates to the third nonexample: instruction is not the same for every group.

Guided instruction is more that just doing one lesson five times. Lessons that work that way can be saved for large-group instruction. Guided instruction means that each group may be working at a slightly different pace or with variations in content. At this time, differentiating instruction takes center stage (Tomlinson, 2003). Finally, guided instruction is not "every day, with every student." It's not likely that you could meet with every group on a daily basis, especially at the secondary level. Instead, you are meeting with each group one to three times per week, depending on the length of the lessons. It's likely that you are going to stack the deck a bit to meet with some groups more frequently, because they need more support. You can also alter the size of the groups, so that those who need more help have fewer members, allowing you more "face time" with them.

Key Features of Guided Instruction

A hallmark of guided instruction is that the dialogue between teacher and learners is carefully crafted following the principles of scaffolding. This term was coined as a metaphor for describing the temporary supports (in the form of questions, cues, and prompts) a teacher offers a learner to help him or her bridge toward a skill or concept he or she cannot do or understand independently (Wood et al., 1976). Teachers of young children use a different phrase: "helping kids with the tricky parts." We like the metaphor of a dance, in which one partner leads while the other pays close attention to the signals and cues being received. The leader in this case is the learner, and the role of the teacher is to respond to the subtle cues that signal understanding and misunderstanding. This is not to say that all is left to chance. Indeed, effective scaffolding requires that the teacher possess expert knowledge about the cues themselves and the level of knowledge they likely represent. It's a bit like being a detective, constantly formulating hypotheses based on students' successes and missteps.

A basic assumption of guided instruction is that the student is responding in a perfectly logical manner, given what he or she knows and doesn't know at that particular moment. Therefore, the guiding question we ask ourselves is this: "What does his answer tell me about what he knows and doesn't know?" For instance, if a student reads "horse" instead of "house," a hypothesis can be formed:

- The child understands many consonant sounds.
- The child may not be attending closely to the word.
- The child may not yet be attending to the medial position in the word.
- The vowel combination may be unfamiliar.

That rapid hypothesis formulation must now be followed by a teacher response. The possibilities include these statements:

- *Telling:* "That word is *house.* Read it again, please."
- *Scaffolding:* "Look again. Does that sound right?" (not attending to print)
- *Scaffolding:* "You missed the middle sound. Look again at the middle letters and try it again." (having difficulty with medial positions)
- *Scaffolding:* "The letters *ou* make the /ow/ sound. Try the word again using that sound." (unfamiliar with this vowel combination)

The problem with telling the child the word right away (the first example) is that you never get to test your hypothesis. By scaffolding your prompts, you have the opportunity to test your hypotheses and thereby gain a better understanding of what the child knows and doesn't know. Our colleague Patricia Kelly puts it another way: "It's saying the right thing to get the student to do the cognitive work."

Scaffolds can be further categorized based on the level of information they provide. Bernie Dodge (1998), the developer of the WebQuest approach to inquiry learning on the Internet, describes scaffolds as a function of the instructional tools students use. We find that his conceptualization of scaffolds can apply to the language prompts we use with students in guided instruction. He describes scaffolds as having a reception, transformation, or production function (Dodge, n.d.). Reception scaffolds direct a learner to a source of information, while transformation scaffolds ask a student to utilize the information to create a new form. Production scaffolds require the learner to create something completely new. We see these as being increasingly complex in nature, and each offers a different level of support. Figure 3.1 offers a comparison of these scaffolds.

Another key feature of guided instruction is that it is based on formative assessment. Students are grouped and regrouped based on their performance, not how the teacher perceives their ability. The most effective guided instructional events are based on formative assessments that are directly linked with the content standards under investigation. For example, if the class is studying literary devices, a formative assessment might explore a student's ability to recognize these devices and to use these devices while writing. The assessment results could then be used to form groups based on identified needs. One group might need further instruction in the difference between foreshadowing and flashback, whereas another group might need instruction in using personification to humanize something not human.

Figure 3.1

Scaffolding types and examples

Type of Scaffold and Task Complexity	Definition	Learning Tool Example	Language Example
Production • Low level of support • High level of task complexity	Learner produces something new with the information.	Templates	"Based on the graph, what do you believe they should do next?"
Transformation • Moderate level of support • Moderate level of task complexity	Learner manipulates information.	Graphic organizers	"Use the bar graph to arrive at your answer. What does it tell you?"
Reception • High level of support • Low level of task complexity	Learner applies information.	Textual and visual information	"Look at the diagram at the bottom of the page to answer."

Assessments are used in school for a number of reasons, including the following:

- To assist student learning
- To identify students' strengths and weaknesses
- To assess the effectiveness of a particular instructional strategy
- To assess and improve the effectiveness of curriculum programs
- To assess and improve teaching effectiveness
- To provide data that assist in decision making
- To communicate with and involve parents (Kellough & Kellough, 1999, pp. 418–419)

These seven purposes can be organized into three main assessment types: diagnostic, formative, and summative. In general, diagnostic assessments are used to identify student weakness or students who may qualify for special programs. Formative assessments are those that teachers use to plan subsequent instruction. Summative assessments are evaluative and typically high-stakes; they are designed to summarize what a student has learned. According to the National Council of Teachers of Mathematics' (2000) *Principles and Standards for School Mathematics,*

> Assessment should be more than merely a test at the end of instruction to see how students perform under special conditions; rather, it should be an integral part of instruction that informs and guides teachers as they make instructional decisions. Assessment should not merely be done *to* students; rather, it should also be done *for* students, to guide and enhance their learning. (The Assessment Principle, ¶1)

In the gradual release of responsibility model of instruction, the use of formative assessment is critical. Guided instruction is dependent on good formative assessment information. It's how teachers form groups and decide what to teach to these groups. We also know that the systematic use of formative assessment data improves student achievement. For example, Black and Wiliam (1998) analyzed the findings from 250 journal articles and book chapters and concluded that the regular use of formative assessments raises academic achievement.

Those frequent formative assessments mean that grouping arrangements change often as well. Groups in traditional classrooms are usually formed structurally, meaning that they are based on some kind of placement test (often the previous year's standardized test scores), with students working in a group for the year with similarly achieving students. Thus, the range of achievement within a classroom is narrowed, and instruction follows placement. Classrooms that use formative assessments to flexibly group students use a situational process, meaning that students are taught first and then grouped for reteaching or extension based on the most current formative assessment. Mason and Good (1993) compared the effects of both approaches on mathematics learning with 1,700 intermediate students and found that learners in the situational approach outperformed those in classrooms that used a structural approach. As classroom teachers, we also rely on another signal that we've gone too long without regrouping: when we call the name of one student for guided instruction and three others stand up at the same time because they have become conditioned to always being grouped together!

Finally, guided instruction provides teachers with an excellent opportunity to differentiate instruction. As Tomlinson (2003) has taught us, we can differentiate content, process, and product. The guided instruction phase of the gradual release of responsibility model allows for differentiation of all three components identified by Tomlinson. First, during small-group instruction, we can vary the content. We can change the texts students are reading. We can change the mathematics problems students are expected to complete. Or we can vary the rate of learning or extend the content beyond what others are learning, allowing for an enriched curriculum for students who have already mastered the grade or course expectations. We do not assume that the same students always participate in accelerated learning or have less difficulty with the text. Rather, these instructional decisions are predicated on formative assessments. One way to ensure that the same students aren't de facto grouped the same way for each unit is to include interest groups as part of guided instruction.

In addition to content, we can differentiate the process we use in guided instruction. For example, we can vary the types of prompts we use, based on the needs of students. Similarly, we can differentiate the questions we ask or the level of support we provide. We can also increase or decrease the visual support that is provided or encourage students to talk with one another in their home language. Some students may benefit from books on tape. Others may need access to the increasing number of textbooks that come with a CD-ROM of spoken text. Still other students may benefit from having content pretaught to them before the focus lesson, so that they will have prior knowledge to draw upon. We have had great success with offering "previews of coming attractions" in the form of graphic organizers or other visual displays so that learners possess a general schema in advance of the unit.

Finally, we can differentiate the products we expect from the guided instructional event. For some students, a conversation with the teacher does the trick. For others, they need to read and write. For still others, a performance or project really allows them to demonstrate what they know. The key to differentiating products is to create choice through a menu of items for demonstrating mastery. This also gives the teacher time to consult with students about their choices, including encouraging them to stretch beyond their comfort zone. Teachers can categorize products according to the following types and then require that each student complete at least one from each category over the course of the semester:

- Oral language (e.g., meet with the teacher; tutor a classmate)
- Written language (e.g., write an essay, a lesson plan, or a poem)

- Performance (e.g., deliver a public speech; write and perform a skit)
- Project (e.g., research a topic; create a visual representation or model)

Based on the products that students have chosen, the guided instruction component becomes a time when students are grouped according to the category—an interest group of sorts.

Instructional Strategies for Effective Guided Instruction

Guided Reading

Guided reading is an instructional approach where small groups of similarly performing students meet with the teacher to read new text. Fountas and Pinnell (1996) describe the purpose and process this way:

> The teacher introduces a text to this small group, works briefly with individuals in the group as they read it, may select one or two teaching points to present to the group following the reading, and may ask the children to take part in an extension of the reading. The text is one that offers the children a minimum of new things to learn; that is, the children can read it with the strategies they currently have, but it provides opportunity for a small amount of new learning. (p. 2)

As with the principles of guided instruction, students are purposefully grouped according to their instructional needs and are taught to apply reading processes they are learning to novel situations—in this case, unfamiliar books. The teacher uses this time to analyze how effectively students are using those reading processes, to help individuals when they get stuck, and to form hypotheses about what students know and don't know. The teaching points come after the reading and are chosen based on those hypotheses. For example, a group of students may be having difficulty reading fluently; thus, the teaching point becomes "making it sound like talking." A guided reading group that still doesn't have directionality of print figured out might have a short lesson on using their fingers to move left to right under the print.

Ms. Cotton calls five of her kindergarten students to the reading table to read *Dad* (Rigby, 2004), a guided reading book for emergent readers. As the students settle in, Ms. Cotton allows them to warm up with a familiar text they have read several days ago. Once they have finished, Ms. Cotton introduces them to the new story, showing them each page and talking about the events that take place. "This story is about a dad who is very busy, taking care of his family." She shows them the illustrations of a man driving a car, planting a garden, and swimming in a lake. At times she uses the language of the text: "Dad is driving." She does this to prepare them for the sequence of ideas that will take place, because she wants to see how well they will do with the pattern of the text. Each sentence begins "Dad is __." She has done several focus lessons on left-to-right directionality, C-V-C words, and basic sight words, and now is the time for students to apply these skills and strategies with unfamiliar text. She also wants to see how well they comprehend, so she has not shown them the last page where Dad is sleeping in a hammock.

She directs individual children to begin whisper reading, staggering start times so that they do not fall into a choral reading of the text. Ms. Cotton moves around the table, listening to each student read, pausing to ask questions or offer prompts when they encounter difficulty, and making anecdotal notes. She notices that the children have done well with moving across each page and have correctly used the pattern of the text. After they finish, she decides to focus on comprehension, asking them to retell what occurred in the story. One student, David, stumbles in his retelling, so Ms. Cotton invites him to use the book to recall. She then asks about the last page—why was Dad sleeping? A minute or two of discussion among the children, with prompts from Ms. Cotton, and the group has arrived at a decision: Dad was sleeping because he was tired from doing so many activities all day! Satisfied that this group is progressing in using their emergent knowledge of phonics, sight words, concepts about print, and comprehension, she sends them back to their collaborative learning groups and reviews her notes about their progress. She will use what she has learned to develop the next lesson for this group.

Guided reading was originally conceived as an instructional approach for elementary students, but many secondary English teachers employ a similar structure for working with their students. Often, guided reading groups at the middle and high school level meet to address literary devices, reading comprehension, vocabulary, and critical literacy.

Mr. Tangaroa has introduced the paradox as a literary device used by writers and storytellers across the world. He has chosen several statements for his focus lesson in order to model his thinking as a reader who becomes aware that he has just encountered a statement that seems to contradict itself yet somehow reveals a deeper truth, such as "being cruel to be kind" or George Bernard Shaw's comment that "youth is wasted on the young." He also has demonstrated how he uses inferencing to unearth the unstated truth. Now Mr. Tangaroa wants students to examine the paradox in the context of poems. As a group of six high school students sits down at the table with him, they receive a copy of a very short poem by John Donne (1572–1631), which reads:

I am unable, yonder beggar cries,
To stand, or move; if he say true, he lies.

Mr. Tangaroa has selected this group of students because he has assessment evidence that they are experiencing difficulty making the kinds of inferences necessary to understand a paradox. He has modeled inferences a number of times and knows that this group of students needs guided instruction. To help them read between the lines, he asks them each to read the poem aloud. He then asks them to talk with a partner about the meaning and why the author would say that the beggar was a liar.

Through prompts and cues, Mr. Tangaroa leads his students to understand the unstated paradox. During their conversation, one of the students finally writes in his journal, "By speaking, the beggar was moving, and so he was lying." Mr. Tangaroa later meets with another guided reading group, this time using the Robert Frost poem "Nothing Gold Can Stay." The first line's statement that "nature's first green is gold" is a more accessible paradox for students to understand, as it does not use a Middle English style and refers to a more familiar phenomenon. By adjusting the relative difficulty of the text, this English teacher can address inferencing and a literary device across a range of learners.

Guided Writing

Like guided reading, guided writing involves the teacher working with small groups of students, based on their assessed performance. During guided writing, students apply what they have learned from focus lessons and collaborative learning with varying degrees of support from the teacher (Frey & Fisher, 2007c). The best guided writing lessons are linked to the focus lessons. For example, if a series of focus lessons centered on word choice, then the guided writing lessons would focus on prerequisite skills or extension opportunities related to word choice.

During guided writing, teachers often use sentence or paragraph frames. These frames, models, or templates help students internalize conventional structures (Fisher & Frey, 2007c). Ms. Allen uses paragraph frames to help her students internalize academic writing. As part of the unit of study on characters, Ms. Allen meets with a group of students who are having difficulty with character summaries and analysis. She presents the paragraph frame in Figure 3.2 to her students and asks them to read it aloud, adding information orally based on the book they are reading.

Figure 3.2

Character analysis paragraph frame

_____ is one of the characters in the story. _____

is _____ and lives _____ (With whom? Where?).

At the beginning of the story, _____ is _____, but _____

who _____. _____

faces a problem when _____

_____.

_____.

_____ attempts to solve the problem by _____

_____

but _____.

Finally, _____ is able to solve the problem by _____

_____.

At the end of the story, _____ has learned that _____

if _____ , then _____

_____.

As she listens to her students, she stops individual students and provides additional cues and prompts. For example, as she listens to Arturo add details about a character named Marty from *Shiloh* (Naylor, 1991), Ms. Allen asks him to list words to describe Marty at the beginning of the story. Arturo says that Marty is shy and that he plays by himself all the time. Ms. Allen asks Arturo what else he remembers about Marty, and Arturo shrugs his shoulders. She says, "What about Marty always looking around for things. What's he doing while he's by himself?" Arturo and Ms. Allen agree that Marty was curious. Ms. Allen lets Arturo continue reading and adding details orally and turns her attention to Isabel, who is stuck in what her character Esperanza from *Esperanza Rising* (Ryan, 2000) has learned. As they complete the task of reading the paragraph frame aloud and adding details from their books, Ms. Allen asks the students to use the frame to construct a paragraph in their journals. Arturo writes:

> Marty is one of the characters in the story. He is 8 years old and lives with his family in a house in the country. At the beginning of the story, Marty is a curious but shy boy who likes to play by himself. Marty is faced with a problem when he finds a stray dog. He knows who the dog belongs to and does not want to return him. He attempts to solve the problem by lying to his family and friends, but then he is caught. Finally, he is able to solve the problem by working hard and treating the dog's owner with respect. At the end of the story, he has learned that if you are honest and treat others with respect, then people will respect you.

Guided writing and the use of frames, models, and templates are not limited to use in the elementary school classroom. College composition experts Gerald Graff and Cathy Birkenstein (2006) recommend the use of frames (they call them templates) as an effective way for developing students' academic writing skills. They defend the use of frames or templates as follows:

> After all, even the most creative forms of expression depend on established patterns and structures. Most songwriters, for instance, rely on a time-honored verse-chorus-verse pattern, and few people would call Shakespeare uncreative because he didn't invent the sonnet or dramatic forms that he used to such dazzling effect. . . . Ultimately, then, creativity and originality lie not in the avoidance of established forms, but in the imaginative use of them. (pp. 10–11)

Student Think-alouds

Think-alouds are commonly thought of as being a teacher-directed instructional practice, as evidenced in the previous chapter. Indeed, it is a powerful tool to make thinking transparent to a group of learners. However, the real goal of a think-aloud should be that students are able to do the same thing—that is, to uncover their own thinking processes as they learn and understand a concept (Wilhelm, 2001). Student think-alouds are conducted in much the same way that teacher think-alouds are done. As the student reads a piece of text or performs a task, she pauses to explain her thinking, including decisions she is making about what to do next. They are ideally suited for guided instruction, as it is an opportunity to listen to the thinking processes of your students as they engage in new learning.

Ms. McDonnell's 6th grade history/social science students have been introduced to the Code of Hammurabi during a focus lesson. When Ms. McDonnell reads their "ticket out the door" written summaries at the end of that class, she notices that several of her students had difficulty in explaining the pros and cons of the laws of ancient Babylon. She decides to meet with this group to review excerpts from their social studies textbook, asking them to think aloud as they read. She hopes that by doing so she will gain insight into their reasoning. She begins by distributing the text and quickly reviewing the significance of this earliest pre-served record of law, and then she asks them to think aloud about their impressions of fairness as they read.

Alex reads the portion of the code containing the *lex talionis,* better known as "an eye for an eye, a tooth for a tooth."

"Stop there, Alex, and tell me how you understand that term," she asks.

"Well, I guess I've got this picture in my head of a judge tak-ing someone's eyeball out because the other guy lost his. Pretty gross," replies Alex.

Ms. McDonnell encourages him to continue reading and think-ing aloud. Alex reads that the law only applied to injuries suffered by a free man, not enslaved people or children.

"I'm thinking that that doesn't seem very fair, like some peo-ple don't count. Girls and stuff," remarks Alex. "Shouldn't there be an 'eye for an eye' rule for everyone?"

Ms. McDonnell asks Alex, "What did you do there just now? When you were thinking aloud?"

He pauses, then states, "I asked myself a question about being fair."

"Exactly! That's how you start to form opinions about pros and cons. Make note about that on your T-chart. Ricardo, how about if you think aloud about the next section, about family laws?"

The students continue in this fashion for the next 10 min-utes, reading parts of the text and commenting aloud about their thought processes. At the end of the lesson, each student has some ideas noted for the pros and cons of the Code of Ham-murabi and will be able to return to the collaborative learning groups to contribute to a project on the importance of these laws on civilization.

Misconception Analysis

The National Research Council's (2005) meta-analysis of the practices that make a difference in history, mathematics, and science instruction for secondary students yielded three main recommendations:

• Teachers must know and anticipate misconceptions students possess about the concepts being taught

• Educators must teach for factual knowledge in a systematic way

• Students must be taught to be metacognitively aware of their learning

The research record is rich on the importance of anticipating misconceptions (e.g., Guzzetti, Synder, Glass, & Gamas, 1993). For example, young children may believe that multiplication always yields a larger number, thus becoming confused when multiplying fractions. Science students may hold a misconception that the Earth is at the center of the universe, or they may confuse acceleration and speed. Anticipated misconceptions are first addressed in focus lessons that are designed to interrupt flawed thinking, such as using math manipulatives to show what occurs with fractions, or demonstrating a series of experiments on a skateboard to highlight the difference between speed and acceleration. Some misconceptions may not be anticipated and may only surface during guided instruction when the teacher has a chance to hear students' reasoning.

Mr. Sanchez has been working with a science class on the concept of volume and has asked small groups of students to explain what occurs when he does a series of demonstrations for them. He asks them to create a definition of volume and records their explanation that volume is the amount of space something takes up. He then places a heavy block into a pan of water filled to the top and asks the six students to discuss why some water spilled over the edge. Their discussion is on target, as all of them are able to describe the displacement effect. He then asks them how they would measure the volume of the block, and Antonio immediately says, "You have to multiply! It's length times width times height!" The others nod in agreement, and soon they have calculated the volume of the block.

Mr. Sanchez then asks them to predict what will occur when he repeats the experiment with objects of varying size, all irregularly shaped. Again, they are able to explain that each object displaced a different amount because the amount of space it took up varied.

"How could I figure out the volume of an object?" he asks.

The group is quiet, not quite sure how to answer. "Let's think about it for a moment. What do you know so far?"

Claudia offers that the water has to go somewhere, and it gets pushed out of the pan.

Maureen reminds the group that they know how to do the math. "We multiply the width and the length and the height."

Antonio now asserts that they need to measure the object, just as they did with the block. Mr. Sanchez didn't expect this; he thought they would surmise that measuring the amount of water displaced would give them the information they needed. He allows them to wrestle with this problem for several minutes, knowing that they need to conclude on their own that their methodology is flawed. He asks them questions from time to time, scaffolding their understanding of the problem they have created for themselves. Claudia is the first to arrive at the notion that they can use the water to determine the volume of an irregularly shaped object. Mr. Sanchez then resumes the lesson he had originally planned, coaching them through the process of measuring the water. However, since this group had more difficulty than he expected, he asks them to write a short explanation of why their first idea did not work, rather than a description of the experiment, as he had originally planned. He will use their writing to check for understanding and to plan for his next guided instruction group with these students.

Formative Assessments in Guided Instruction

As we have stated earlier, formative assessments are critical in order to check for understanding as students begin to take on new concepts, skills, and strategies. A number of examples have been described in this chapter; we will augment them with other ideas. In guided reading, the teacher used anecdotal notes and observations as she listened to her students read. Another formative assessment for guided reading with emergent and early readers is the running record, a system for recording the reading behaviors used during an oral reading. This written record is analyzed later by the teacher to determine the systems a child is using well, partially, or not at all, especially as they relate to knowledge of letters and sounds, the syntactic structure of the language, and meaning cues. Although the details of gathering and analyzing running records are beyond the scope of this book, excellent resources abound (e.g., Clay, 2000).

For older readers, informal reading inventories, which are commercially prepared grade-level passages, can be administered several times per year. This information is useful, but it does not provide the immediate feedback needed to check for understanding. Retellings are an excellent tool for measuring the extent to which a student has comprehended the reading. Retelling rubrics are included in many reading programs and are often a part of a district's bank of informal assessments.

Guided writing yields a permanent product, which serves as a great information source. Again, holistic or trait-specific rubrics are useful for analyzing writing. Because it can be unwieldy to analyze every piece of writing, we teach our students at the beginning of the year how to use student-friendly rubrics to score their own writing. Student rubrics are useful for building a learner's understanding of the expectations and measures of success that need to be internalized. Student self-scoring also increases metacognition, as learners are able to witness their gains over time (Fisher & Frey, 2007b).

Student think-alouds are a bit trickier to assess because the product—talking—is so transient. The best way to capture this information is to prepare a simple checklist of what you are listening for (the purpose), such as reading comprehension strategies or critical thinking skills. As a student thinks aloud, you can note the qualities that he included and have a record of what he did not do. Over time, patterns may emerge, and this checklist can help you create learning objectives for future guided instruction. We have included a sample checklist in Figure 3.3.

Misconception analysis is about noticing the thinking that students are doing and matching that to correct and incorrect assumptions. Anecdotal notes are best for capturing this information. We keep a notebook divided by student name at our guided instruction tables so that we can record our observations as they arise. Because it is not always possible to predict when a misconception might occur, we have made it a habit to jot a few notes on these pages at the end of each guided lesson. It's too easy to lose the details in the rush of the day, so our notebooks remind us to take this time.

Figure 3.3

Student think-aloud checklist

Think-aloud Element	Thinking Skill Used	Example
Comprehension	• Makes connections • Visualizes • Questions text • Makes inferences beyond the text • Determines importance • Summarizes	
Content knowledge	• Activates background knowledge • Uses word derivation • Applies new knowledge	
Evaluation	• Offers opinions • Speculates • Seeks other sources • Notices what has been left out	

Conclusion

Guided instruction serves as a linchpin between the modeled instruction that students have received and the independent performance they will need to eventually complete. The demand on the teacher is high during this phase, particularly because these lessons are subject to quick changes in direction, depending on where the learners lead you. Students are typically grouped with other learners who are similarly performing, based on assessment information, but the groupings change frequently due to ongoing formative assessments. The guided instruction phase is an ideal time to differentiate instruction by content, process, or product, because the small group sizes allow for much higher levels of customization. The goal of guided instruction is precision teaching that ultimately increases the rate of learning because students do not have to learn again what they already know or try to fill in missing gaps on their own. The art and science of teaching come together in this phase as the teacher responds to the nuances of understanding exhibited by each student.

4 | CHAPTER

Collaborative Learning: Consolidating Thinking with Peers

A significant body of evidence suggests that regardless of the subject matter or content area, students learn more, and retain information longer, when they work in small groups (Beckman, 1990; McInnerney & Roberts, 2005; Slavin, 1980, 1983; Totten, Sills, Digby, & Russ, 1991). Students who work in collaborative groups also appear more satisfied with their classes, complete more assignments, and generally like school better (Johnson & Johnson, 1999; Summers, 2006).

Collaborative learning provides students an opportunity to work together to complete specific tasks. Sometimes these tasks are developed by the teacher, and other times these tasks are initiated by students. Regardless, collaborative learning tasks offer students an opportunity to work together to solve problems, discover information, and complete projects. The best collaborative learning tasks allow students to apply what they have learned in focus lessons and guided instruction. Less effective collaborative learning tasks are those that are disconnected from the course of study or topic. These less effective collaborative, or cooperative, tasks have been allowed to flourish, which is why we believe teachers rarely employ this component of the gradual release of responsibility model of instruction.

A dilemma that many teachers face is what those collaborative activities might be. We would argue that many of them are right under our noses, so to speak. Consider your own experiences with whole-group activities that require less direct involvement from you. For example, showing a film in class is nearly always done with the whole class, while the teacher spends the time hushing students, redirecting their attention to the screen, and otherwise monitoring behavior. This isn't teaching; it's managing. Your expertise is not being used. Instead, you are acting much like a movie theater usher. This is an activity that can be reconceived as a collaborative activity such as a listening and viewing station. Six students with headphones can watch a film segment together, take notes, and respond to discussion questions while you are delivering guided instruction to another group. Thus, your expertise is being maximized to the benefit of your students. Anytime you find yourself managing, rather than teaching, ask yourself whether the activity could be recast as collaborative learning. Other examples of times teachers fall into the manager role include supervising independent work tasks such as completion of grammar workbooks, supervising students as they respond to a writing prompt, observing peer response and feedback groups, and overseeing whole-class independent reading.

What Collaborative Learning Is Not

First and foremost, collaborative learning is not the time to introduce new information to students. New information should be introduced during focus lessons and should be reinforced during guided instruction. As you might expect, students become frustrated with collaborative learning when they are not sure what to do.

Collaborative learning is also not simply "group work" in which a single product is produced for the group. A group project may be useful for some types of learning, but the gradual release of responsibility model of instruction requires that each student produce a product as a result of the interaction. Not only does this accountability ensure that students engage with the task, but it also provides teachers with a formative assessment tool, a way to check for understanding and determine next steps that meet instructional needs. These next steps can, of course, be addressed during subsequent focus lessons and guided instruction events.

Collaborative learning is also not ability grouping. In fact, collaborative groups must be purposefully constructed to ensure maximum success. Success in a collaborative group is dependent on students having access to peers with diverse ideas, interests, and skills (Sapon-Shevin, 2007). As such, mixed-ability groups, purposefully organized by the teacher, are important. Asking a group of students who don't speak much to work together will not likely produce the desired outcome. Similarly, assigning a group of students who all can complete fraction problems to a spiral review task will likely result in their off-task behavior. Although this group of students can probably use the spiral review, they are more likely to complete the tasks when they feel like they are working with others who need some assistance, guidance, or explanation.

A body of research on the work of same-ability small groups has found that high-achieving and low-achieving homogeneous groups do not work together effectively, because the high-achieving groups failed to interact with one another, whereas the low-achieving groups did not have the resources within the group to complete tasks successfully (e.g., Bennett & Cass, 1988; Webb,

1982). Low-achieving females appear to be particularly at risk for marginalization in this type of grouping arrangement (Mulryan, 1995). Interestingly, Bennett and Cass's (1988) study found that heterogeneous groups were more successful when they were constructed so that the number of low-achieving students outnumbered the high-achieving ones within the group. This combination ensured that the high-achieving students did not take over the learning process and exclude the low-achieving members in the rush to complete the task.

Teachers use three types of grouping patterns in their classrooms: teacher-choice, student-choice, and random. There are specific reasons for each of these grouping practices. Teacher-choice is the most appropriate grouping pattern for guided instruction and collaborative learning. The teacher can ensure that students are selected for guided instruction based on their assessed needs. Similarly, the teacher can ensure that students work in mixed-ability groups during collaborative learning. Student-choice for grouping is most appropriate for extended tasks such as projects outside the classroom. When students choose their group members for these types of projects, they are more likely to complete the tasks. Random grouping also has a role in the classroom, especially to ensure that students have the opportunity to interact with each member of the learning community. Random groups are especially useful for book clubs, discussion groups, and other times when sharing ideas, reactions, reflections, beliefs, or feelings is the focus.

Key Features of Collaborative Learning

As we discussed in the chapter on guided instruction, teachers should spend a significant amount of time each day with small groups of students. The key is to keep the rest of the class engaged in meaningful activities during this time. It is important to keep this goal in mind. In some classrooms, students engage in collaborative learning all at the same time, and the teacher walks around the room managing the environment. This isn't the best use of the teacher's time, because this period could have been spent in guided instruction. When students have been taught the routines and procedures for collaborative learning, they require less supervision.

In addition to noting the time investment for teaching students the routines and procedures, a number of researchers and practitioners have identified essential features necessary when students collaborate with one another. The following five features should be considered in any collaborative learning task (Johnson, Johnson, & Smith, 1991).

• *Positive interdependence.* The first feature focuses on the interconnectedness of the learning situation. Each member of the group must be important for the overall success of the endeavor. Collaborative tasks are not simply individual work completed with peers. The structure of the task should require that each member of the group offer a unique contribution to the joint effort. In this way, students consolidate their thinking, explain processes to one another, and learn as they do so.

• *Face-to-face interaction.* Students have a number of opportunities to collaborate with one another in the digital and virtual worlds, but it is important that the classroom provide students an opportunity to interact with one another face to face. In these interactions, students should teach one another, check each other's understanding, discuss concepts and ideas, and make connections between the content and their own lives.

• *Individual and group accountability.* As noted before, individual and group accountability are critical components of effective collaborative learning. Students must understand the products that are expected from the collaborative learning event. One of the ways to ensure that students remain focused on accountability is to keep the size of the group small. The smaller the size of the group, the greater the individual accountability is likely to be. In addition to individual accountability, groups should be accountable for completing tasks. These tasks can vary from something as simple as rewinding the videotape at the completion of the viewing to something as complex as writing a group summary of the information learned during the lesson.

• *Interpersonal and small-group skills.* For groups to work effectively and efficiently, each member must possess and use the requisite social skills. Often, specific skills such as leadership, decision making, trust building, turn taking, active listening, and conflict management must be taught.

• *Group processing.* A final feature involves the group members themselves discussing their progress and what they might do to improve their productivity or working relationships. This is a critical, yet often neglected, component of collaborative learning. This processing allows students to reflect on their actions and learning and to recommit to their studies. Over time, and with practice, students can ensure that their collaborative learning tasks are meaningful and fun.

Instructional Strategies for Collaborative Learning

Reciprocal Teaching

Reciprocal teaching is an instructional strategy in which groups of four students read a piece of text and then engage in a conversation about the text (Palincsar & Brown, 1984). The conversation is structured by the use of four strategies: summarizing, question generating, clarifying, and predicting. As with most collaborative structures, students need practice and modeling before they can use reciprocal teaching with their peers. For reciprocal teaching to be most effective, students must understand the four comprehension strategies that make up the conversation (Oczkus, 2003):

• *Summarizing* is a brief written or oral review of the main points of the text. Text can be summarized across sentences, paragraphs, or the selection as a whole. When students first use reciprocal teaching, they are typically focused on sentence- and paragraph-level summaries. As they become skilled with procedures, they begin to summarize at the paragraph and passage levels.

• *Questioning* focuses students on inquiry and investigation. As students generate questions, they identify the type of information that is important enough to provide the basis for a question. They then pose this information in question form to their peers. During the questioning portion of a reciprocal teaching discussion, students often answer each other's questions and thus engage in conversations that extend beyond the text. Over time and with modeling and practice, students can be taught and encouraged to generate questions at many levels of complexity. For example, students might learn to ask the four types of questions common in question-answer relationships (Raphael, Highfield, & Au, 2006), including "right there," "think and search," "author and you," and "on your own."

• *Clarifying* is a metacognitive activity in which students learn to notice things that they don't understand. During the discussion about the text, they ask for clarification on components of the text that blocked their comprehension. Early in the use of reciprocal teaching, students often seek clarification on individual words. Over time, they will also clarify ideas that confuse them, missing background information that others might have, and unfamiliar experiences discussed in the text. In addition, with modeling and practice, students will incorporate another comprehension strategy—visualizing—into their clarifying. One of the ways that readers clarify confusing information is to "make a movie" in their mind as they read.

- *Predicting* is a process of making an educated guess, based on the best information available, about what might happen next. To make predictions successfully, students must activate both background and prior knowledge, pay attention to what the author has said, and make inferences. Predicting also keeps readers engaged with the text as they want to read further to determine whether their predictions are correct.

Mr. Nelson's 4th grade class is focused on health. Through a series of focus lessons and guided instructional events, the students in this class are learning about nutrition, exercise, and fitness. On one particular day, students are working in collaborative groups using reciprocal teaching. Each group has a different piece of text to read and discuss while Mr. Nelson meets with small groups to discuss personal fitness plans. One of the groups is reading *The Food Pyramid* (Petrie, 2003). As expected, they use summarizing, clarifying, question generating, and predicting to read and discuss this text. Interestingly, this text generates more questions for the group than anything else. As each student takes turns questioning, the group identifies several items for further inquiry, including the following:

- What is a healthy food item? An unhealthy food item?
- Why is it important that we eat healthy food?

- How many food items did we eat last night that were considered healthy? Unhealthy?
- Do you think you are eating healthy meals according to the food guide pyramid?
- What might you want to change to eat better?
- Is it possible to eat better? At home? At school?

To generate one product from this collaborative activity, Mr. Nelson asks students to select one question for further study. Angel selects the final question, "Is it possible to eat better at home and at school?" She begins her quest for the answer on the Internet and then reads through additional texts looking for possible answers. Over the weeklong investigation of their questions, students draft responses, meet with Mr. Nelson for editing sessions, meet with peers for feedback, and read extensively. Angel's answer is complex and reads, in part:

> It is possible to eat better, if you want to and if adults help. With some education, parents and cafeteria staff could prepare very healthy meals. This would mean that students would have to stop begging for unhealthy meals, like fried food. To eat healthier, students need choices and they need to make good choices.

Listening/Viewing Station

As noted earlier in the chapter, a listening or viewing station can replace the traditional whole-class film. This approach frees the teacher up from acting as a manager rather than instructor. Following the viewing, students can discuss the content together and respond to prompts individually. This group and individual accountability fosters participation by all members, rather than the one or two students who are willing to complete the assignment for everyone.

Ms. Cheong, an 8th grade physical science teacher, has been teaching her students about forces and motion. They have been learning about the effects of unbalanced forces on changes in velocity. She knows that this concept is more fully understood when students see such an effect in action, so she has assembled a series of film segments that illustrate it. Groups of six students watch a 15-minute film clip Ms. Cheong has prepared from the PBS (2007) *Nova* documentary "Avalanche!" Ms. Cheong previously introduced the reading titled "Elements of a Slide" during a focus lesson to build the students' background knowledge about avalanches (PBS, 2007). When students arrive at the station, they each complete an anticipation guide featuring 10 statements, some true and some false. They watch the film clip (using headsets so as not to disturb other groups) and follow along with a printed transcript of the tape (which PBS provides at no cost). Their task is to analyze the film segment for details about the physics of an avalanche. Using a note-taking guide, students discuss and respond to a series of questions about the role of various forces, including the slope of the mountain, wind, sound waves, and weak layers of snow within the snow pack. Each student then returns to his or her anticipation guide, responding again to the 10 true/false statements.

Ms. Cheong uses a group-reward process for fostering collaboration among the groups. After completing each group task, students take short quizzes on the material featured. The quizzes are completed individually, with points awarded to groups where all members have achieved a passing score. The quizzes themselves are differentiated to address the needs of some students in the class who are working at different levels. Thus, each group has a vested interest in making sure that all members of the group understand the material. These short quizzes also provide Ms. Cheong with formative assessment information about each student's progress.

Visual Displays

Creating visual displays, or graphic organizers, is another way for students to consolidate their understanding. Visual and graphic displays require that students represent the relationships among facts, terms, or ideas. Graphic organizers are also known as concept maps, knowledge maps, story maps, advance organizers, or concept diagrams. A significant body of research indicates that the use of visual and graphic displays facilitates understanding (Alvermann & Boothby, 1986; Clements-Davis & Ley, 1991; Fisher, Frey, & Williams, 2002; Moore & Readence, 1984). The key is to have students construct the visual display. Having students fill out photocopied graphic organizers, after they understand their basic functions, is a waste of time and minimizes the task to a worksheet. What students need instead are opportunities to collaborate with their peers in constructing visual displays that make the connections between ideas and information transparent.

Ms. Tran uses a collaborative poster, a form of visual display, with her geometry students to teach them the process of proofs. Each group of four students is given a different task, or proof, to solve. Each member of the group receives a different colored marker and is required to sign his or her name on the back of the poster. This step ensures that each student contributes to the poster and is accountable for the information on the poster. During their discussions, students apply what they have learned about proofs during focus lessons and guided instruction, including the process that has been modeled for them several times:

72

1. Identify or generate the statement of the theorem.
2. State the given.
3. Create a drawing that represents the given.
4. State what you're going to prove.
5. Provide the proof.

Although the modeling of this process of solving proofs is critical and the guided instruction students receive can be used to correct misconceptions and address knowledge gaps, it is the collaborative learning task—in this case, the visual display—that requires students to use what they know.

The idea of a collaborative poster for the geometry class can be modified for different grades and subject areas. For example, a group of 1st graders might use a Venn diagram to identify the similarities and differences between two characters. A group of 6th graders might use a time line to aid their understanding of the various kingdoms and dynasties in Egyptian history. And a group of biology students might use a process chart to organize their understanding of cell division.

Literature Circles/Book Clubs

Literature circles (Daniels, 2001) and book clubs (Raphael, Pardo, & Highfield, 2002) have been popular approaches for differentiating texts among readers. Book clubs have been used more widely in elementary classrooms, while literature circles have been implemented with greater frequency in intermediate and secondary classrooms. The element both have in common is peer-led small-group discussions of a common text. Students do not read in the presence of others (they do so during independent reading or at home); they gather together to discuss what they have read thus far. The literature circles approach stresses choice and the temporary nature of the groups, as the configurations change with the next round of books. Several principles are central to literature circles (Daniels, 2006):

• *Students have choice in the books they read.* These choices are often limited to the list the teacher has compiled (usually chosen because they have a common theme and represent a range of text difficulty), but the student chooses which title he or she will read, sometimes with some "artful teacher guidance" (p. 11). Group formation is then predicated on book choice, so the groups function as interest groups.

• *Students have a responsibility to themselves and to their peers.* These responsibilities include record keeping, contributing to group discussions, and, of course, keeping up with the readings. They create the ground rules for the group and design a schedule of the times they will meet. Once comfortable with the process, groups jointly determine how much will be read before the next meeting; it becomes much harder to hide in a group of six or so when you have not done the agreed reading.

• *Increased engagement occurs in these peer-led discussions.* Daniels calls this quality "airtime," and it stands to reason that in a small group the level of participation is going to increase (p. 11). Drawing a quiet student into the discussion becomes the job of supportive peers, not the teacher.

The social development of these groups can be challenging for some students, who may have come to rely on teacher-directed instruction to the exclusion of any responsibility for their own learning. Many teachers initially use role sheets to formalize the social and academic behaviors necessary for effective peer-led discussions. These roles typically align with the content of the discussion, such as discussion director, vocabulary enricher, and so on. Once students become adept at literature circle discussion, these formal roles are abandoned in favor of a more natural ebb and flow to the conversation.

Ms. Johnson's 5th grade students have been participating in literature circles since the beginning of the school year and are now in their fourth cycle. Each cycle features a unifying essential question, to be answered through the whole-class shared reading Ms. Johnson does with everyone in her focus lessons, and one of the five literature club titles read in collaborative groups. The essential question for this cycle is "Why do some people act bravely in the face of danger, while others do not?" Ms. Johnson is reading *Anne Frank: The Diary of a Young Girl* (Frank, 1993) to the entire class, and the students are reading one of the following:

- *Sacajawea* (Bruchac, 2001)
- *Stealing Home: The Story of Jackie Robinson* (Denenberg, 1990)
- *Chief: The Life of Peter J. Ganci, a New York City Firefighter* (Ganci, 2003)
- *Harvesting Hope: The Story of César Chávez* (Krull, 2003)
- *Voices from the Fields: Children of Migrant Farmworkers Tell Their Stories* (Atkin, 2000).

Ms. Johnson has selected these books carefully to represent a range of possible reasons for bravery, including righting an injustice, saving the lives of others, and venturing into new realms. She has considered gender, ethnicity, and age, as well as text difficulty (two of the selections are picture books). She previewed each title during a book talk, and students made their top three selections. This process allowed her to shape the groups and to match a few students with books that were not significantly above their reading level.

For two weeks, literature circles have met to discuss the readings and then write their reactions in their reading journals. Jessica's group is reading *Harvesting Hope,* and they have ended each discussion by revisiting the essential question to see whether they have developed an answer. At the end of the two weeks, each student writes an essay about the question, using examples from their literature circle selection and *Anne Frank.* Jessica's essay contains the following paragraph:

> I think people are brave and not brave for lots of reasons. Anne was brave because she felt like she had to be to survive. She wasn't a sad girl, and she stayed brave on the outside even when she was scared on the inside. She knew it made it easier for her family, too. César Chávez was brave for a different reason. He knew what was happening was wrong. He didn't like seeing so many people he cared about being treated that way. So he stood up for everyone. Maybe Anne and César had one thing in common about being brave. They both cared about other people.

Labs and Simulations

Labs and simulations are another way that students can apply what they have learned in focus lessons and guided instruction. Labs and simulations are an ideal structure for collaborative learning. The problem with most labs and simulations is that they are used with the whole class at the same time, and thus the teacher does not have an opportunity to engage in guided instruction. Instead, labs and simulations should be used with some students at a time so that the teacher can also work with groups of students in guided instruction.

Labs are most common in science education, but they can also be used in art and physical education. In science classrooms, students should "participate in a range of lab activities to verify known scientific concepts, pose research questions, conceive their own investigations, and create models of natural phenomena" (National Research Council, 2006). Participating in these types of activities, especially in a gradual release of responsibility model of instruction, helps students understand.

In Mr. Miller's science class, students are applying what they have learned about electricity in a lab. Students have been provided with several pieces of fruit and vegetables (lemons, potatoes, grapefruit, tomatoes, oranges), shiny copper pennies, zinc-plated screws, wires with alligator clips, a light-emitting diode (LED) with a low-voltage rating, and an electronic instrument called a multimeter. The collaborative task is to consolidate the knowledge gained thus far and to light the LED. Once the group has successfully delivered electricity to the LED, they are instructed to use the multimeter to measure the amount of electricity produced. Thus, the task is twofold: first, use the supplies to make electricity, and then determine which arrangement produced the most electricity.

Importantly, Mr. Miller does not simply walk around the room to manage this lab. He knows that this is the ideal time for him to provide guided instruction and push students' thinking to higher levels. He calls four students to the corner of the room to share the Eyewitness book *Electricity* (Parker, 2005). He asks these students to turn to page 22, as he wants to review circuits and conductors with this group. From their formative assessment, he knows that these four students do not fully grasp the concepts of circuits and conductors and will thus have difficulty with the lab.

Nearby, one of the groups has inserted a penny into one side of the lemon and a zinc-plated screw into the other. They connect the wires to the penny and screw and then light the LED. Mr. Miller looks up and asks the members of the group whether they can make their signal strength any stronger. He also reminds them that they *each* have to explain, in their science journals, why this has worked. Part of Andrew's notes say:

> When the screw contacted with the citric acid in the lemon, it started two chemical reactions: oxidation and reduction.

Like labs, simulations are used to ensure that learning is applied (Aldrich, 2005). Simulations are common in social studies, language arts, and other content areas for learning such things as cause and effect. Simulations International (www.simulationsintl. com), a global company that provides simulation consulting, design, and development, identified five elements of simulations. If the following five elements are present, then the activity qualifies as a simulation:

- The simulation itself is not real, but aims to mimic reality.
- The simulation contains a mathematical or rules-based model.
- Time is continuous.
- Where you are is always a consequence of what you have done in the past.
- Where you are going is completely your choice. (www. simulationsintl.com/simtypes.html)

In her government class, Ms. Fink uses simulations of town hall meetings and congressional voting. During one session, she provides students with a scenario very real to their lives—drag racing on the freeway. She distributes copies of a newspaper article about drag racing, a political cartoon on the subject, a section of the vehicle code, and a proposed amendment to the code, which criminalizes observers of drag racing. The room is charged, and students begin sharing their opinions about this with one another. Ms. Fink interrupts their conversations and reminds them of the process of a town hall meeting.

She distributes role sheets, including mayor, council members, community members, parents of a young adult killed while drag racing, business owners, observers of drag races, three well-known drag racers, and police officers. Ms. Fink reminds her students that the conversation can go in any direction they chose, as long as they respect the town hall process and remain in their roles. In their collaborative groups, students share their thinking about the proposed law and provide each other feedback and commentary.

During this time, Ms. Fink meets with specific students who need additional support to make their position known. She also meets with the mayor and council members in a small, guided instruction group to remind them of their role in the discussion and how to operate the town hall meeting. Over several days, with focus lessons, guided instruction, and collaborative learning events, the students are ready for the simulation.

Janae starts the conversation:

> Dear Mr. Mayor and members of the council. I can't believe that you're thinking of making it a crime to watch drag racing. What could I, the observer, do? Where will it stop? Will it be a crime to observe a house robbery? Will it be a crime to watch someone run a stop sign or light? And who will enforce this rule?

Playing the role of a business owner, Marvin asks to speak next.

> I like drag racing, so it doesn't matter what rules you make up. . . .

Ms. Fink interrupts the group, reminding students that they must be true to their role, and says to Marvin, "Which business owner's perspective are you speaking from? You need to think about that. Some business owners might believe what you just said; others would disagree with you. Maybe you should start over and introduce yourself. That would give us the context for your speech."

Over the course of the town hall meeting, many different opinions are expressed, ideas are changed, and positions are forwarded. Ms. Fink knows that her students have been prepared for this simulation because of the structure of her classroom and the work she has done to prepare them.

Jigsaw

In this collaborative learning structure, group members are each assigned some unique material to learn and then teach to other group members. Elliot Aronson first used the jigsaw approach in 1971 in Austin, Texas. He developed it in response to the fighting that was occurring as a result of desegregation. In most classrooms at the time, students competed against one another for grades and had few opportunities for, or motivation to, collaborate. In restructuring the class for positive interdependence, Aronson recalls a comment one of his colleagues said to a group of students as they were teasing a group member: "Talking like that to Carlos might be fun for you to do, but it's not going to help you learn anything about what Eleanor Roosevelt accomplished at the United Nations—and the exam will be given in about 15 minutes" (Aronson's account of the history of the jigsaw approach can be found at www.jigsaw.org/history.htm).

Jigsaw can be used across grade levels and content areas. Aronson's original work was conducted in a 5th grade classroom. Jeff Niemitz (a geology professor from Dickinson College) uses the jigsaw technique in a class of 120 undergraduates to introduce the topic of igneous rock classification. The steps of the jigsaw are fairly straightforward:

- As students enter the auditorium, they each pick up one rock from a box of samples by the classroom door. The box contains samples of gabbro, granite, and basalt.
- The instructor asks students to study their rock samples and write down all the observations they can make about them.
- After giving students several minutes to study their rocks, the instructor asks the students to make groups of three so that each group has three different rock types.
- Each group then compares rocks, noting similarities and differences. The instructor then asks groups what they have noted in their rocks and writes down responses on an overhead transparency.
- Students make all of the observations that one might expect them to make about color, grain size, and texture, providing an engaging base for the instructor to then introduce igneous rock classification.

Skills Practice

Students need time to practice new concepts in the company of peers who are learning along with them. This is especially true of actions that require many repetitions in order for the skill to move to a level of automaticity. For instance, young readers need to acquire higher levels of automaticity to support more fluent reading (LaBerge & Samuels, 1974). The same can be said for memorization of computational math facts in addition, subtraction, multiplication, and division. Goldman and Pellegrino (1986) state that "the importance of drill on components is that the drilled material may become sufficiently over-learned to free up cognitive resources and attention. These cognitive resources may then be allocated to other aspects of performance, such as more complex operations like carrying and borrowing, and to self-monitoring and control" (p. 134). Memorization of math facts, sight words, letter names, and such are typically done in whole-group drills or independent work. However, students often perceive these activities as tedious and do not engage in the activity, thus failing to develop the necessary automaticity.

It is important to note that automaticity is not merely rote memorization, because the learner must be able to activate the skills consciously when needed, such as when solving a math problem or reading a book. That is, they must be able to retrieve the information when needed. Collaborative learning arrangements offer an ideal time for students to practice these skills in the company of peers while the teacher works with other students. The combination of oral and written language channels helps contribute to students' rates of acquisition because it accesses more than one element of communication.

Ms. Guest uses collaborative centers daily to reinforce concepts taught during focus lessons and guided instruction. She has a word study center where she rotates various skills, including sight words, digraphs and consonant blends, and word families. Her 1st grade students have been working on onset and rime patterns in one-syllable words. Four or five heterogeneously grouped students meet at an easel she has posted low to the floor. The chart on the easel has a number of common rime patterns ending in consonant blends (e.g., -act, -arn, -arm, -elt). The children have markers and paper of their own to write on, as well as a large bucket of magnetic letters. They work together to create new words by combining the magnetic letters with the rime patterns. Members of the group take turns making new combinations, and the entire group chants the new words. Each child has an individual task as well. Their paper is arranged as a T-chart, with one column labeled "Words" and the other labeled "Nonwords." Ms. Guest doesn't just want her students to decode; she also wants them to consider the meaning of the words they are creating. Their task is to sort the words they have created into these two categories, which also generates quite a bit of discussion.

Teisha: My word is *darn, d-a-r-n.*

All: Darn.

Teisha: It's a real word. I'm writing it in my real word list.

Carla: Naah, it's not a word!

Teisha: Ya-huh! *Darn* is when you fix a sock.

Carla: It's not a word! You made that up.

Arturo: It's a word. My mama says darn when she messes up. "Darn it!"

Carla: When she fixes a sock?

Controversies aside, Ms. Guest likes using collaborative activities for skills practice because her students say each word or math fact aloud, read it, and write it. The individual worksheets also give her insight into the relative vocabularies of each child, which serves as an excellent formative assessment.

Formative Assessments

As with each phase of the gradual release of responsibility framework, checking for understanding is essential. Doing so can seem to be more of a challenge in collaborative learning because so much of the activity is taking place outside the presence of the teacher. Yet the key to gathering this formative assessment information is to design individual accountability within the group work. The students in the reciprocal teaching example chose a question for further research on the Internet and produced a report. The students who viewed the video together turned in anticipation guides and took a short quiz on the material. The geometry students developed a collaborative poster so that the teacher could determine the level of participation for each member. The literature circle students wrote in their reading journals after each meeting and wrote a final essay at the end of the cycle. The students in the science demonstration lab were required to complete a lab sheet, while the students who participated in the court simulation had a performance and public speaking task. Even the young students in the skills practice center had a permanent product to turn in—their list of words and nonwords.

These are the guiding questions we use in designing formative assessments for collaborative learning:

- What evidence do I need to make future instructional decisions?
- What evidence would be most useful for guided instruction follow-up?
- Does this assessment task provide meaningful feedback to the student?
- Can every member of the group do this assessment task in a meaningful way?
- If no, in what ways can this assessment task be modified to meet the needs of those students?

Conclusion

Collaborative learning provides a critical bridge in student learning because it allows novice learners to refine their thinking about new concepts and skills. The oral language development in such settings is particularly valuable because it requires the use of social and academic language in order to accomplish the task. Individual accountability is a hallmark of collaborative learning because it minimizes the frustration felt by some students who believe they have shouldered an unfair burden. The configuration of the group is important to its success. Although student choice or interest groups are useful at times, in most cases the grouping should be heterogeneous so as not to impoverish some groups who have fewer collective resources among them. This point is just as important for high-achieving students, who tend to collaborate less in groups they perceive as needing less of their help.

5 | CHAPTER

Independent Learning Tasks:
Not Just "Do It Yourself School"

The final phase of the gradual release of responsibility model of instruction focuses on independent learning tasks. As Candy (1991) notes, independent learning is both a goal and a process: a method of learning and a characteristic of learners. As we will discuss in the next section, independent learning is not simply photocopying worksheets for students to complete. We agree with Marcia Tate (2003), who says, "Worksheets don't grow dendrites" (p. 1). Instead, independent learning tasks need to provide students with opportunities to apply what they have learned through focus lessons, guided instruction, and collaborative learning. Independent learning should also help students become increasingly self-directed and engaged.

Phil Race (1996) of the University of Durham suggests that all learning is essentially independent learning. That is not to say that teachers don't play a profound role in students' learning. It just means that we must ultimately ensure that students take responsibility for their learning. We can do this through the materials we provide, the supports and scaffolds we offer, and the feedback we communicate to our students. As evidence of the ubiquitous nature of independent learning, Race offers the following examples:

- When students learn from our lectures, much of the actual learning takes place after the events, in ways that have all the hallmarks of independent learning.
- When students learn through practical work, most of their learning is done under their own steam, even while using the people around them (fellow students, tutors, and support staff) as resources to help in their learning.
- When students learn from learning resource materials, whether in libraries, learning resource rooms, or at home, most of their learning is done independently, at their own pace, and in their own way.
- When students learn from open learning materials, they are essentially learning at their own pace and in their own ways from materials specially prepared to activate their desire to learn, giving them the chance to learn by doing, and providing them with feedback on their efforts.
- When students learn from each other, they can still be regarded as learning independently in many respects; they are not then dependent on the presence of tutors. Indeed, the ways in which students learn from each other have all the hallmarks of independent learning, in that students have choice of how to use each other and how to structure the times, places, and rates at which such learning takes place. (Race, 1996)

Race's examples clearly communicate the range of possibilities for independent learning tasks. Before we explore what independent learning is *not* and then the key features of independent learning, we should remember that independent learning is in fact the goal of schooling. As Saskatchewan Education (n.d.) notes, independent learning

- Is based on meaningful learning activities.
- Enables individual learners to take responsibility for their own learning.
- Is essential for lifelong motivation and growth.
- Prepares students for their role as responsible citizens in a changing society.

What Independent Learning Tasks Are Not

As we have noted, independent learning tasks are not just a pile of worksheets handed to students to complete. It should not be, as some students say, "death row by dittos." As Pincus (2005) notes, many worksheets are not very interesting, require practice on skills that students already have mastered, take time from teaching to score, and often lack purpose, especially a purpose that is directly connected with the focus of the lesson. That's not to say that all worksheets are bad. Summers (2004), for example, demonstrated the ways in which worksheets can be used in science. In her example, the worksheet was clearly connected with a focus question, a trip to a science center, and teacher instruction. To ensure that worksheets are used appropriately, Pincus (2005) identified three questions that teachers should ask themselves as they consider the use of a worksheet for independent learning:

1. Does the worksheet aim at a research-based goal?
2. Does the worksheet employ effective and efficient means to reach that goal?

3. How can this worksheet best be used: for instructional modeling, for guided practice, or as a pre- or post-test (and if so, what does the teacher learn)? (p. 76)

A second thing that independent learning should not be is rote memorization. As Levstik and Barton (1997) note, the rote memorization of isolated facts fails to advance students' conceptual understanding. Similarly, Willis (2005) argues that rote memorization is inconsistent with what we now know about how the brain learns. We even now understand that rote memorization of mathematic facts—something we have all taken for granted—isn't as important as teaching students to explain, justify, predict, compare, and derive ideas in mathematics (O'Brien & Moss, 2004). In other words, independent learning tasks should allow students to apply information, not just regurgitate it (Diaz-Lefebvre, 2004).

Finally, independent learning is not necessarily silent. Although independent learning is focused on the individual, it does not require solo work. We know that people learn in a variety of ways, that there are multiple intelligences or multiple ways of being smart (Gardner, 2006). As such, the independent learning tasks we encourage should respect the various ways that humans think, learn, and process information.

Key Features of Independent Learning Tasks

Independent learning should allow students a "direct encounter with the phenomena being studied rather than merely thinking about the encounter, or only considering the possibility of doing something about it" (Borzak, 1981, p. 9). This view is consistent with the thinking of Kolb (1984), who forwarded a theory of experiential learning. He and his colleagues (e.g., Kolb & Fry, 1975) suggested that learning occurs through one of the following four ways and that each person probably learns best through just one way:

- Concrete experience
- Observation and reflection
- Abstract conceptualization
- Active experimentation

Carl Rogers (1969) identified several principles of learning, which are helpful in our discussion of independent learning.

1. Human beings have a natural potential for learning.

2. Significant learning takes place when the subject matter is perceived by the student as having relevance for his/her own purposes; when the individual has a goal he/she wishes to achieve and sees the material presented to him/her as relevant to the goal, learning takes place with great rapidity.

3. Learning which involves a change in self-organization—in the perception of oneself—is threatening and tends to be resisted.

4. Those learnings which are threatening to the self are more easily perceived and assimilated when external threats are at a minimum.

5. When the threat to the self is low, experience can be perceived in differentiated fashion and learning can proceed.

6. Much significant learning is acquired through doing.

7. Learning is facilitated when the student participates responsibly in the learning process.

8. Self-initiated learning which involves the whole person of the learner—feelings as well as intellect—is the most lasting and pervasive.

9. Independence, creativity, and self-reliance are all facilitated when self-criticism and self-evaluation are basic and evaluation by others is of secondary importance.

10. The most socially useful learning in the modern world is the learning of the process of learning, a continuing openness to experience and to incorporating into oneself the process of change.

These 10 principles suggest that independent learning tasks need to be meaningful, experiential, and relevant. These principles also indicate that both the teacher and the student have a role in learning, a proposition supported by research and our experience. In fact, we would go so far as to say that the teacher—specifically, what the teacher does—is the most significant variable in student achievement.

Instructional Strategies for Effective Independent Learning Tasks

Independent Learning Centers

As Farmer (1994) notes, an independent learning center is a space in the classroom with resources where students can pursue independent projects. These independent learning centers allow students to use their reading, writing, and research skills and to focus on topics that interest them. They align with standards in that the materials at the independent learning center can be based on the content at hand. In addition, they provide students an opportunity to authentically use their literacy skills.

In her 3rd grade classroom, Ms. James uses an independent learning center to focus her students' thinking about the sky. She knows that her students have lots of questions about this unit of study. She also knows that, despite her best efforts to address them, her students have a number of misconceptions about the fact that objects in the sky move in regular and predictable patterns. During both her language arts and science periods, she reads aloud and thinks aloud about texts. She guides her students' thinking during small groups and plans a number of experiments for them in collaborative learning groups.

However, Ms. James knows that her students need opportunities at an independent learning center to ask and answer their own questions. For several weeks, the materials at the center focus on the moon. A number of books are available at various reading levels about the moon, lunar cycles, and moon exploration. There are also poems and short stories about the moon. Ms. James knows that pairing fiction and nonfiction texts facilitates understanding of both (Camp, 2006). In addition, the independent learning center includes many pieces of equipment for simulating the phases of the moon as well as illustrations and photographs in which the appearance of the moon changes.

As students interact with the information at the independent learning center, they ask a variety of questions. Michael asks, "How does the moon stay up in the sky?" while Adrienne asks, "Is there light on the moon?" and Jacob asks, "Can there be two full moons in a row?" These questions deepen students' understanding of the content standard for 3rd graders while also encouraging inquiry, self-directed learning, and engagement with the topic under investigation.

Independent learning centers can also be used with older students. For example, in their physical education class, students have been encouraged to develop personal fitness plans. Coach Bronson has provided a range of materials at the independent learning center for their use, including fitness books, fitness magazines, diet information, and health information. In addition, the center includes information on high blood pressure, heart disease, tooth decay, muscle pain as a result of exercise, and just about any resource students might need to develop and implement their fitness plan. Coach Bronson knows that the focus lessons, guided instruction, and collaborative learning activities he has provided as part of his class will help students think about fitness and nutrition. He understands that students will have to own this information and make personal decisions to use it. He also understands that students will require different information at different times, and that many of his students do not have access to this type of information at home. For Coach Bronson, the independent learning center offers an excellent opportunity for his content information to be used. As Teresa says one afternoon, "Coach, I need more information about sugar and fat. I'm really into this now and wanna get into shape. You got any more stuff for me?"

Sustained Silent Reading and Independent Reading

Teachers spend significant amounts of time teaching students to read with the hopes that reading becomes a lifelong habit. We hope readers read for information and enjoyment. We know that reading is a skill necessary in the workplace. Can you imagine a doctor, lawyer, electrician, mechanic, engineer, nurse, police officer, or other professional who didn't need to read every day to be successful at work? In addition, we know that these professionals read widely; they don't just read from one source.

It seems reasonable to suggest, then, that reading be part of the school day. To develop this habit, students need to practice it regularly. We don't think that practice makes perfect, but we do hope that practice makes it permanent. And we want to create permanent readers. As such, one of the independent learning tasks students should engage in on a daily basis is reading or, as the students in Gay Ivey and Karen Broaddus's (2001) study called it, "just plain reading." Teachers have two ways to ensure that their students read regularly: sustained silent reading (SSR) and independent reading.

Sustained Silent Reading. Setting aside time to read every day is a fairly simple thing to do. Making it meaningful is a bit more complex (Fisher, 2004). The idea behind SSR, and other initiatives that allow students time to read at school, is that students must complete the phases of the gradual release of responsibility in reading. Neglecting the independent learning phase results in students with isolated skills who do not regularly read for information and pleasure. To us, it would be the same as teaching a child to ride a bike without ever letting the child outside to just ride.

Pilgreen (2000) identified eight factors necessary for SSR programs to be effective. A summary of each of these factors is presented in Figure 5.1. Our experience suggests that teachers and schools can use these eight factors to self-assess their readiness for an SSR program and to determine the necessary changes to ensure that student reading develops into a permanent habit.

Independent Reading. As with SSR, students read on their own during independent reading. However, unlike during SSR, they read from books selected on a specific topic, such as motion and matter, DNA, causes of World War II, food-borne illness, or their literature club book selection. That is not to say that there isn't choice during independent reading. Quality independent reading initiatives involve a number of books on a topic, and students choose from those books. Independent reading should mirror the behaviors of real readers who read widely for information. We also know that independent reading builds background knowledge and fuels vocabulary growth.

For example, Ms. Rodriquez knows that her 8th grade social studies students need to read widely to understand the early and steady attempts to abolish slavery in the United States. Ms. Rodriquez uses the textbook for her focus lessons and guided instruction. She employs a number of simulations recommended

Figure 5.1

Eight factors of SSR success

1. **Access.** This principle deals with getting reading materials into the hands of students, which Pilgreen sees as the responsibility of the teachers and the schools. This involves more than simply telling students they must bring something to read.

2. **Appeal.** This factor deals with student interests, the variety and range of materials we offer to our students, and, yes, even making sure that the materials we offer are "classroom appropriate."

3. **Environment.** This has to do with physical comfort, alternatives to the traditional classroom setting, and the possibilities of reading as a social interactive activity for those students for whom reading in silence is not conducive to the freedom associated with SSR.

4. **Encouragement.** This includes modeling, discussions, and postreading opportunities for sharing, and enlisting parent support and involvement.

5. **Staff training.** Providing training in SSR, answering organizational and "how to" questions, and encouraging all teachers to provide a specific set daily time for SSR are discussed.

6. **Nonaccountability.** While students are not required to complete the usual types of formal assessment, such as book reports or tests of content knowledge, SSR practices do provide for informal accountability through opportunities for sharing in discussion, writing, or other formats.

7. **Follow-up activities.** SSR, Pilgreen says, needs to provide ways for students to "sustain their excitement about the books they have read" (2000, p. 16). Activities and shared experiences are very effective in encouraging further voluntary reading.

8. **Distributed time to read.** Habits—including the habit of reading—are formed through sustained efforts over time. Occasional lengthy periods of time set aside for free reading are not as powerful as shorter periods of 15 to 20 minutes at least twice a week.

Source: From "Book Review: *The SSR Handbook*" (pp. 434–435), by H. M. Miller, 2002, *Journal of Adolescent & Adult Literacy, 45.* Copyright 2002 by the International Reading Association. Reprinted by permission.

in the text, as well as reciprocal teaching, vocabulary centers, and viewing stations, for collaborative learning. However, she knows that her students need to read widely if they are to understand the diverse perspectives on this topic. As such, she has assembled (with the help of her school librarian) more than 50 readings on this topic. Some are picture books; others are Web sites printed out and placed in protective sheets; others are memoirs, poems, speeches, and so on. Each day, students read for 10 minutes from these selections. In doing so, they build their knowledge base on this content standard. Importantly, they use what they have read before to understand as they read. It's a cumulative process in which students become increasingly knowledgeable about the content.

A comment by Britney highlights this point:

> I got it more and more each day. But when I read about her experience in Ohio, I really started to understand how hard it was to stop slavery. Let me show you. [She produces a copy of a Web page.] Sojourner was at a meeting, and here's what happened [reading]: "At the end of the meeting, a man came up to her and said, 'Old woman, do you think that your talk about slavery does any good? Do you suppose people care what you say? Why,' continued he, 'I don't care any more for your talk than I do for the bite of a flea.' 'Perhaps not,' she responded, 'but, the Lord willing, I'll keep you scratching.'" You see what I mean? It wasn't easy. You couldn't just change the laws. People had really bad opinions. They really believed it. Today it's easy to say how terrible and wrong it was, but they didn't see that it was a violation of the Constitution.

As is evidenced by Britney's understanding, independent wide reading helps students contextualize and understand the content. In an effort to transfer more responsibility to students, Sheri Sevenbergen, a teacher at Hoover High School in San Diego, California, developed a self-assessment rubric for her students to use during independent reading (see Figure 5.2). This rubric allows students to reflect on their independent reading and to make changes accordingly.

Writing to Prompts

Writing is thinking, and independent thinking at that. When we write, we continually monitor our understanding. As such, writing-to-learn prompts are an excellent independent learning task. As Fulwiler and Young (1982) explain

> Writing to communicate—or what James Britton calls "transactional writing"—means writing to accomplish something, to inform, instruct, or persuade. . . . Writing to learn is different. We write to ourselves as well as talk with others to objectify our perceptions of reality; the primary function of this "expressive" language is not to communicate, but to order and represent experience to our own understanding. In this sense language provides us with a unique way of knowing and becomes a tool for discovering, for shaping meaning, and for reaching understanding. (p. x)

A number of writing-to-learn prompts have been identified (see, e.g., Fisher & Frey, 2007b), including the following:

- *Entry slips:* a prompt posted on the board for students to respond to upon entering the classroom. For example, upon entering their 4th grade classroom, students might be asked to respond to the prompt "Describe, in great detail, Martha's journey thus far in the covered wagon."
- *Yesterday's news:* a prompt designed for students to summarize information. For example, after reading about the life cycle of various insects, students are asked to respond to the prompt "Yesterday's news: My life cycle is complete."

Figure 5.2
Independent reading rubric: A self-evaluation guide

What Kind of Reader Was I?

Name: _____   Period: _____

	4—Exceptional	3—Proficient	2—Progressing	1—Developing
Reading Behaviors, Materials Selection, Engagement/Attitude, Accountability	• I read the whole time. • I respected the readers around me. • I have "just right" material ready to read. • I rarely need help from my teacher. • I knew my reading was not making sense and I did something to fix it. • I frequently talked to myself in my head about the story. • I used word strategies whenever I couldn't pronounce (decode) the word.	• I read most of the time. • I respected the readers around me. • I usually have "just right" material ready to read. • I sometimes knew my reading was not making sense and I did something to fix it. • I sometimes caught myself thinking as I was reading. • I sometimes used word strategies whenever I couldn't pronounce (decode) the word.	• I just read part of the time. • I read too fast. • I was off-task about half the time. • I wasn't careful when I selected my books. • I wasn't paying attention to my thinking as I was reading. • I skipped over the tricky words and didn't try to figure them out. • I distracted the readers around me. • I got up a couple of times during independent reading time.	• I was looking around the room or staring into space instead of reading. • I was pretending to read most of the time. • I did not pick "just right" books. • I didn't understand what I was reading. • I didn't think as I was reading. • I got up a lot for no reason. • I did not respect the readers around me. • I wasted my learning.

	4—Exceptional	3—Proficient	2—Progressing	1—Developing
Reading Behaviors, Materials Selection, Engagement/Attitude, Accountability	• I slowed my reading down when I was reading a confusing part and reread it. • I stayed in my reading space the entire time. • I felt great about myself as a reader. • I set high reading goals for myself, and read as much as I can during independent reading. • I always complete my reading log correctly. • I volunteer to ask about and recommend reading materials to others.	• I sometimes went back and reread when it didn't make sense. • I moved around during independent reading. • I frequently recommend reading materials to others. • I usually complete my reading log after independent reading.	• I rarely recommend reading material to others.	• I never recommend reading materials to others.

Source: Sheri Sevenbergen, Hoover High School, San Diego, CA. Used by permission.

- *Crystal ball:* a prompt designed to elicit a prediction. For example, during an experiment in a chemistry classroom, students are asked to respond to the prompt "Crystal ball: What will happen when we add this agent to the solution?"
- *Exit slip:* a prompt to be completed before leaving the classroom. For example, before leaving class for the day, students in world history are asked to respond to the prompt "The best thing I learned today was . . . ."

The most flexible prompt used for independent writing is called a RAFT prompt (Santa & Havens, 1995). In addition to focusing students on the content they are studying and helping them develop their writing skills, the RAFT prompt teaches students about perspective. RAFT stands for

Role—Who are you as the writer?

Audience—To whom are you writing?

Format—What form will the writing take?

Topic—Who or what is the subject of this writing?

During their studies of U.S. presidents, students in Anthony Brown's 5th grade class have learned about Victoria Woodhull, a leader of the American women's suffrage movement, who in 1872 declared that she would run for president of the United States. During the focus lesson, Mr. Brown read aloud the book *A Woman for President: The Story of Victoria Woodhull* (Krull, 2004). As part of their independent learning tasks, Mr. Brown has asked his students to select a RAFT prompt and respond. He offers the following choices:

Role—Reporter
Audience—Readers of the 1870s

Format—Interview
Topic—The presidency

Role—Husband
Audience—Victoria
Format—Personal letter
Topic—Why I'm proud to be your husband

Role—Victoria
Audience—Self
Format—Speech
Topic—Why I should be president

Responses to any of these prompts allows students to clarify their own thinking and Mr. Brown to check their understanding of the content. Writing is a good way for students to engage in independent learning tasks.

Conferring

As we have noted before, independent learning tasks are not necessarily silent, nor are they solo acts. Conferring is an example of an independent learning task in which individual students meet with the teacher or other adult to discuss progress, ask questions, obtain feedback, and plan next steps for independent assignments.

Conferring, as part of the gradual release of responsibility model of instruction, occurs across subject areas. There is evidence of the effectiveness of conferring in reading, writing, mathematics, science, and more (Bomer, 1999; Heuser, 2000; Yeh, 2006). While different experts identify different components necessary while conferring, we appreciate the sage advice from Choice Literacy (www.choiceliteracy.com) as it summarizes the advice on conferring:

- *Let the learner lead.* As with guided instruction, the learner sets the direction. The teacher can have a specific conferring point, such as discussing progress on a research report or giving feedback on an essay, but it is the student who directs the course of the conversation.

- *Know the history of the student.* Here's where all that formative assessment pays off. In addition to general interest inventories, have a folder of assessments and products for each student so that you can refer to items as needed. Students often want to know how they are doing in a class, so this information can be useful.

- *Assume the child has something to communicate.* Don't be deceived by outward signs of reluctance or by the age of the student. Most students recognize that one-to-one conversations are rare in busy classrooms, and they often warm to it after a few conversations. You will sometimes feel as though neither you nor a particular student got much out of a conference. This is the time to examine what was said and not said. What isn't mentioned in the conversation can sometimes speak volumes.

- *Be patient, and respect silence.* No one likes to be rushed in a conversation, and teachers are especially guilty of filling up the silences with their own voices. Give students time to compose their thoughts and to reflect on the conversation. It is amazing how much more they will talk when we remain quiet.

- *Look for the teachable moment.* Paying attention to what the student says—active listening—will reveal a number of teaching points. Although you may not be able to address all of the needs a student has during the conferring session, choose one to focus on. The others can be recorded in your notes for future focus lessons or guided instruction. Remember that turning points in conversations often come near the end, not the beginning. These might be called "doorknob confessions" because they are usually a tossed-off remark as students are leaving the table (e.g., "Oh, yeah, I'm kind of stuck on finding stuff on antibodies, but I'll work it out"). Don't get fooled into thinking that these remarks are inconsequential. Now's the time to invite the student to stay a bit longer while you provide some instruction or guidance.

- *Keep it short.* We keep a timer on our tables to monitor the time—no more than five minutes. It's easy to get caught up in a sociable chat with an outgoing student or to spend a very long time with a student who's got a laundry list of concerns. Schedule another conference for students with more support needs, and watch your time so you can get to all your students.

- *Include follow-up.* Each conference should include specific independent tasks that the student can complete before the next meeting. Before the student leaves, schedule the next conference. This practice ensures that you always have a schedule prepared and notifies the learner that you'll be inquiring about his or her progress at the next meeting.

Ms. Vasquez confers regularly with her 2nd grade students as part of their writing instruction. Her students have been working on a technical writing genre on explaining a process; students call it a "how-to" paper. Ms. Vasquez has done several focus lessons on the format and language style, and they have examined examples of such writing in the form of recipes, board game directions, and instructions on how to create a figure from Legos building blocks. Her guided writing lessons have centered on writing directions for simple classroom tasks, such as turning on the computer and choosing books from the classroom library. Students have worked in pairs to compose a how-to paper on playing a game of their choice, including alerts to the reader on mistakes to avoid. Each child is now independently writing a paper that will be published in a class book. Members of the class have all selected their topic and have been developing their papers. Ms. Vasquez follows up with her first conference with Sara, who has chosen to explain how to make a peanut butter and jelly sandwich. She brings her work to the conference table; Ms. Vasquez reads it over and then asks Sara what she thinks the paper needs.

Sara replies, "I don't know. I keep writing but then I think of new things."

"Like what?" asks Ms. Vasquez.

"Like, I wrote about putting the peanut butter on the bread, but then I remembered that I forgot to say something about a knife."

"Hmm," says Ms. Vasquez. "Let's go back to the paper you wrote with your partner on how to play Twister. It looks to me like you didn't organize your information in the same way."

For the next few minutes, the teacher and her student make columns with the following headings: materials, time needed, alerts, steps, and recommendations. Ms. Vasquez shows Sara how to list the information in each column and reminds her to use this note page as an organizer for her paper. "Maybe this will help you write a new version. Can you do that before our next meeting? Let's talk again on Thursday, and you can show me how it's going," says Ms. Vasquez.

In her Algebra I class, Ms. Sullivan confers with individual students as part of their independent work. She uses information from the formative assessments that she collects to focus the conversation. When they meet with her for the conference, students know to bring work samples to discuss. During a conferring session with Edgar focused on the associative and distributive properties, Ms. Sullivan starts by asking him to explain his understanding of the sample problems. She knows that Edgar is repeating algebra and that he doesn't have an opportunity to receive help at home, as he is the primary caregiver for his younger brothers and sisters. As she listens to him explain how to solve these problems, Ms. Sullivan notices that he is misapplying information and adding numbers with x as if they didn't have x. When there is no variable (x) present, Edgar has the problem correct. For example, for $72 + (70 + 96) = $ ___, Edgar has correctly written 238. However, when a variable is added, the answers are incorrect. For example, for $92 + (78x + 56) = $ ___, Edgar has incorrectly answered $226x$. He doesn't yet understand that he can't add numbers that contain variables unless the variables are the same. Ms. Sullivan seizes this teachable moment to re-explain the rules. Together they quickly work through several examples and nonexamples. She leaves him with a new problem set, organized into two columns, one with variables and one without. She asks Edgar to work on these problems independently so that they can talk about them further before the end of the class period.

Formative and Summative Assessments in Independent Learning Tasks

Conferring is itself a type of formative assessment because it offers a way to monitor progress with students. In addition to conferring, students can complete weekly progress updates to the teacher to report on the status of longer projects, such as those completed in independent learning centers. We typically include these prompts:

- Name of project
- My goal is to be done by [date].
- This week I did the following . . .
- To meet my goal, I still need to . . .
- My next step is . . .
- I might need help with . . .

These updates serve as a good record for students to gauge their progress toward goals they have established, especially with secondary students who sometimes have trouble with procrastination and organization. In addition, they can be useful in parent-teacher conferences when there are discussions about work habits and such.

Creating updates can be cumbersome for very young students, but using stamps to do so works quite well. At the beginning of each week, students are given a list of independent tasks. As they complete each task, they stamp their "job cards" so that they can see their progress toward weekly goals. These job cards are differentiated among students so that individual needs are met. Families also like these job cards because they serve as a weekly update of their child's work, without any extra paperwork for the teacher.

Sustained silent reading poses a special consideration because the evidence shows that procedures such as book reports and reading logs undermine the very things we hope to achieve—namely, improved attitudes toward reading, more time engaged in reading outside the school day, and wider choice of materials that students choose to read (see Pilgreen, 2000, for a meta-analysis of this research). Therefore, formative assessments of sustained silent reading must be conducted in a subtle manner. We administer short reading surveys a few times a year to our students and include questions about their habits, their favorite authors and genres, and their purposes for reading outside school. These data allow us to monitor the ways in which the reading lives of our students change over the course of the year. We also make note of what goes on during SSR time, such as selection habits, reading stamina, and levels of engagement. These factors, too, can lead to individual conferences with those who seem to struggle.

Like conferring, writing prompts also serve as a formative assessment unto themselves. As we have noted in previous chapters, a writing-to-learn prompt is an effective way to check for understanding of the day's lesson. Entry and exit slips can be structured for summarizing, clarification, or prediction. Because these writing-to-learn prompts are brief, the teacher can look through them quickly to gain a sense of what needs to occur next. We don't grade all of these; we use them as part of the participation grade for the class.

You have probably been waiting for summative assessments to be discussed. Importantly, summative assessments occur after independent learning, when students have had ample opportunity to acquire and use information in increasingly independent ways. Summative assessments most commonly take the form of end-of-chapter/unit tests, essays, and projects. Swearingen (2002) describes five conditions for designing good summative assessments:

- *Authenticity.* The summative assessment chosen should reflect not only the content learned but also the way in which it was learned. A science unit with a number of demonstrations and labs should have a task that mirrors that type of performance assessment. The summative assessment for a history unit that featured graphic organizers, for example, should include this type of task on the test.

- *Variety.* By far, the majority of summative assessments are paper-and-pencil tasks, despite the evidence that tells us that this format is not optimal for all students. Create a summative assessment map for the course or subject to accompany the curriculum map, and analyze it for variety. Are there performance assessments and projects in addition to traditional tests? Tiered tests also introduce variety, as students choose from a menu of items.

For example, a tiered summative assessment on decimals might begin with a section that all students are required to answer, followed by a section containing 10 items, with students choosing any 7 to complete.

• *Volume.* The amount of testing that is done seems to grow each year, as state and national tests are developed to assess progress of schools. Many of these tests are conducted in the early fall and late spring, and testing fatigue can set in quickly. Balance these testing schedules against the classroom summative assessments. Nontraditional assessments such as presentations and projects are particularly welcome. Moreover, summative assessments may be significantly reduced in favor of formative assessments during these testing windows.

• *Validity.* This construct is closely related to authenticity— the content of the assessment should match what has been taught. Of course, no one would substitute an essay on the Reformation for a grade in biology, because it is blatantly invalid. But how often have we asked students to write an essay on the content, without ever giving them opportunities to engage in that type of thinking? It is important to remember that validity doesn't apply directly to the test itself but to what we do with the test score. A student who fails on an essay about the Reformation hasn't necessarily failed to learn the content. The format of the test may be working as a constraint. If that is the case, consider another kind of measure, such as an oral explanation.

• *Reliability.* Along with validity, the other major test construct is reliability, which refers to the trustworthiness of the assessment. Therefore, answers deemed correct must in fact be correct, or the test isn't reliable. This consideration applies to other forms of assessment beyond paper-and-pencil tasks. For example, assessments based on rubrics must have a degree of interrater reliability, meaning that your colleagues would score items similarly. Consensus scoring is one way to reach a reasonable level of reliability on major summative assessments like science projects and English essays. To consensus score, student work is collected, and several different teachers read each piece. Time spent with colleagues discussing evidence in student work yields tremendous professional growth and improves the instruments we use for summative assessments.

Conclusion

Independent learning is the time when students fully assume the cognitive load of learning by applying what they have learned to novel tasks. Choice becomes a major feature in this phase of the gradual release of responsibility model, as students engage in active experimentation. Independent learning centers can be organized as a starting point for creating new products. Sustained silent reading and independent reading are times when students consolidate the content they have learned, along with the reading comprehension strategies they are acquiring. Independent writing, especially writing prompts, offer students a chance to extend their understanding. Finally, conferring gives the teacher a way to further personalize learning for each student. Both formative and summative assessments figure into the independent learning phase. As with formative assessments, the summative instruments should be designed around principles of authenticity, variety, validity, and reliability, while also acknowledging the volume of assessment that occurs across the school year.

6 | CHAPTER

Implementing a Gradual Release of Responsibility Model

Perhaps a gradual release of responsibility model describes an instructional design process that is similar to the one you already use in your classroom; for other readers, it may be quite different. The focus of this chapter is on issues of implementation, especially as it relates to a sequence for planning and introducing this model to your students. In addition, we will address what peers and administrators should look for in a classroom structured in this way. Finally, we'll end this chapter with questions to ask yourself as you implement a gradual release of responsibility model.

Although we have presented this framework in a sequential manner, implementation is not a linear process. We rarely march lockstep through a focus lesson, followed immediately by guided lessons for all the students, then collaborative learning, holding independent learning for the very end of the unit. Instead, we view these components as recursive and iterative.

Gradual Release of Responsibility Is Recursive

Throughout each unit of instruction, we purposefully plan for a continuous shift of the cognitive load across time. Therefore, 3rd grade students learning about text features in informational books receive focus lessons on how an expert reader uses headings, titles, and so forth, to create a schema and make predictions about what the author will discuss. They will participate in several guided lessons where they apply their nascent knowledge of text features to books that match their reading levels, as well as guided writing to develop titles and headings for existing informational passages. The students will collaborate in partner reading activities using short articles with text features. Eventually, they will create informational reports on animals they are studying in science, with text features required in their writing. A new unit of study features the same gradual release across time, with focus lessons dominating the beginning of the unit and increasingly more independent learning as the students become more adept at applying the information. In this way, a gradual release of responsibility model can be seen looping through each major unit of instruction.

Gradual Release of Responsibility Is Iterative

Each unit also contains microelements of the gradual release, with each cycle building on the accumulating knowledge of the students. We'll use the language of mathematics to explain the difference between the recursive process we just described and the iterative approach to which we now refer. A recursive function repeats the same algorithm each time using the same sequence, whereas an iterative function "is one which carries out an algorithm many times, the input for each calculation being the result of the previous one" (Brochmann, 2007, ¶5). As with this mathematical principle, a gradual release of responsibility model is predicated on the new knowledge that students are acquiring, so that the teacher might do a focus lesson, followed by a collaborative learning event, then returning to a focus lesson that uses what they have gained collaboratively. Guided instruction may occur the following day for some students, while others are working collaboratively.

Thus, the first two days of a unit in biology might begin with a focus lesson on properties of cells, followed by a collaborative learning activity as students work together to determine whether an egg meets the criteria of a single cell. After students explain their reasoning, the teacher follows with another focus lesson on the single unfertilized cell at the center of the egg, surrounded by proteins that nourish and protect the cell, with students comparing their reasoning with the new information. The following day begins with guided instruction as the teacher meets with small groups of students to apply their new understandings to a reading on the fertilized ovum and its development as an embryo. Meanwhile, other students are engaged in collaborative learning, analyzing a diagram of an animal cell together and entering the information into their science journals.

Gradual Release Is Consistent with Other Research-based Approaches

Our instructional practices have been profoundly influenced by the work of Carol Ann Tomlinson's (2001) differentiation of instruction and by Grant Wiggins and Jay McTighe's (2005) development of Understanding by Design (UbD). We use these processes in developing units of study for our students, and the decisions made through differentiating instruction and UbD are integrated into the gradual release of responsibility model.

Differentiated Instruction and Gradual Release

Tomlinson's framework for differentiation describes a process for considering students' learning styles, abilities, and interests to create educational experiences that balance challenge with success. Tomlinson further explains that these experiences can be differentiated in one or more aspects of the curriculum: content, process, and product. As she and others have noted (e.g., Benjamin, 2002), some educators see the implementation of differentiated instruction as problematic because the reliance on whole-group instruction doesn't allow for ways to create time for students to work at different rates, on a variety of topics, or with a range of materials. The gradual release of responsibility model has been our solution to the logistics of differentiation. The focus lesson phase provides time to build background information and introduce new concepts for all students. It is in the guided instruction, collaborative, and independent learning phases of the framework that differentiation takes place. We can group students homogeneously for guided instruction that is customized to their learning needs, then regroup them heterogeneously for peer learning. At times, collaborative learning also becomes homogeneous, as when students are grouped by interest or task. Learners also work independently to demonstrate their mastery of a concept or skill. Learning contracts, curriculum compacting, and tiered assignments and tests all factor into the educational experiences of our students.

UbD and Gradual Release

The Understanding by Design process developed by Wiggins and McTighe (2005) features three major components:

- Identifying the desired results
- Determining acceptable evidence

- Planning learning experiences and instruction

The backward planning achieved in determining the enduring understandings of learning is invaluable in developing the units of study. In particular, the essential questions posed throughout a unit keep us and our students centered on the purpose of the learning—the first step listed here. The UbD tools also help us plan the assessments we will use—the second step. Finally, the gradual release of responsibility model gives us a framework for the third step in the UbD process—planning learning experiences and instruction. By considering the recursive and iterative aspects of the framework, we have an instructional design process that allows us to plan learning experiences that transfer the cognitive load to students over time, while being able to differentiate those experiences. Of course, the instructional design is meaningless without units of study that possess the rigor of enduring understandings and a clear structure of formative and summative assessments to check for understanding (Fisher & Frey, 2007a).

A Planning Tool for a Gradual Release of Responsibility

Once units of study have been identified, teachers must plan a series of lessons using a gradual release of responsibility framework. The Northview (Grand Rapids, MI) Public Schools, in partnership with the Ball Foundation (www.ballfoundation.org), have been engaged in districtwide study and professional development of the gradual release of responsibility model and have piloted a planning tool for use by teachers in this K–12 district. This planning tool has been useful for fostering collaboration among grade-level and course-alike teachers as they engage in backward planning, curriculum alignment, and differentiated instruction. A copy of the tool that Northview teachers use can be found in Figure 6.1.

We have also included a sample lesson developed in San Diego by middle school math teacher Michael Soriano. He created these lessons to use with his 7th grade pre-algebra students. We'll discuss each aspect of the planning tool using Mr. Soriano's plan as a guide. His completed planning tool appears in Figure 6.2.

Topic/Theme and Standards

The unit of study is on algebra and functions, and these lessons partially address California Mathematics Standard 1.1 on using variables and operations to write equations.

Essential Question

An essential question reminds students of the overarching purpose of learning concepts. In this case, students are reminded to consider the reasons that functions and relations are represented in a variety of ways, as well as how they relate to daily life and technology.

Literacy Connections

Mr. Soriano's school is committed to literacy across the curriculum and includes reading, writing, and oral language activities in each unit. In this case, he has chosen a read-aloud of a picture book that exhibits the principles he is presenting. He has also designed a collaborative poster assignment to foster social and academic language and will use a short-essay written response to the essential question as one of his summative assessments.

Focus Lesson/Direct Instruction/Modeling

Mr. Soriano introduces the concept of inputs and outputs and their relationship to functions by showing students a video game

Figure 6.1

A planning tool for a gradual release of responsibility

Topic/Theme	Standards	Essential Question	Literacy Connection(s)

Focus Lessons/Direct Instruction/Modeling

Guided Instruction

Whole Group	Whole Group	Small Group	Small Group	Small Group	Small Group

Figure 6.1 (continued)

A planning tool for a gradual release of responsibility

Collaborative Learning

Collaboration 1	Collaboration 2	Collaboration 3	Other Concurrent Activities

Independent Practice with Conferring

Practice Task(s)	Student/Teacher Conferring

Assessment	
Formative	Summative

Source: From Northview (Grand Rapids, MI) Public Schools. Used by permission.

Figure 6.2
Sample lesson plan

Topic/Theme	Standards	Essential Question	Literacy Connection(s)
Prealgebra: Input, Output, and Functions	CA 7th Grade MATH 1.1.: Use variables and appropriate operations to write an expression, an equation, an inequality, or a system of equations or inequalities that represents a verbal description	Why are functions and relations represented in different ways?	Read aloud: *Two of Everything* (Hong, 1993) Collaborative poster Essential question short essay

Focus Lessons/Direct Instruction/Modeling

Instructor will show the class an Xbox 360 wireless controller and use that to clarify the meaning of inputs and outputs. "Let's say that you are playing *Madden NFL 07* video game and you are controlling San Diego Chargers football player LaDainian Tomlinson. When you push the B button, L.T. does a spin move. When you push the Y button, L.T. does a stiff arm. Whenever you push a button on a controller, you are inputting a command. The output is what you see on the television. So when you are playing video games, you input a command by pushing the buttons on a controller, then the signal goes inside the Xbox 360, and then it will output the result through the television."

Instructor will explain the analogy between the inputs and outputs of a video game system and the mathematical process of inputs and outputs and show the class an interactive online function machine from www.mathplayground.com/FunctionMachine.html.

Instructor will input random numbers into the machine and the machine will reveal the corresponding output value. Then the instructor will think aloud about how to determine the function inside the machine.

Instructor will read a short story called *Two of Everything* by Lily Toy Hong. The story is about a magic pot that doubles anything that is placed inside it. Before beginning the story, explain to students that there is a function occurring during this story, and that their task will be to identify the function during guided instruction.

Guided Instruction

Whole Group	Whole Group	Small Group	Small Group	Small Group	Small Group
Instructor will create an input and output T-chart. Students will be required to take notes in their notes journal. Instructor will use $y = x + 3$ as the example. The T-chart looks like this:		Convert functions in read-aloud into equations. 1. Create an equation that represents the situation in the story. 2. Identify some of the inputs and outputs from the story. 3. Create an input/output table if the magic box added two after doubling. Ask each student to think aloud as they explain reasoning for arriving at function.	Graph functions using previously learned concepts of domain and range in order to visualize functions as well as understand the algebraic concept. Students bring functions created on interactive function machine to graph.	Misconception analysis guided instruction with identified learners as needed based on formative assessment of student work. Possible misconceptions include: 1. Learner does not recognize a novel function (only previous examples) 2. Learner confuses domain and range variables	Error analysis as needed with identified learners based on difficulty with textbook problems.

x (input)	y (output)
1	4
3	6
7	10
-5	-2

Instructor will explain that $y = x + 3$ is the function rule and that x is the input and y is the output. Then instructor will explain that for every number you input for x, 3 will be added to it and the result is the output, y.

Figure 6.2 (continued)
Sample lesson plan

Collaborative Learning

Collaboration 1	Collaboration 2	Collaboration 3	Other Concurrent Activities
Teams of students use online interactive function machine at www.mathplagound.com/FunctionMachine.html. Students take turns creating and then hiding a function, then their partners input numbers to determine the function. Each partner writes an explanation of how he or she solved for the function.	Peer problem-solving session to solve problems in math textbook on page 565, #4–6, 7–10, 17–20. Students use different colors of ink to denote their contribution to the work.	Make a collaborative poster of a function machine you have created to perform a real-world math task. Be sure to include the inputs and outputs and explain the function used by the machine. Include a graph to visually represent the function in a different manner.	Continue work on your independent project on graphing in your daily life. How do you encounter graphs throughout your week? Use the materials in the independent learning center for more information about types of graphs; graphs in science, social studies, art, and physical education; and different ways that information is reported.

Independent Practice with Conferring

Practice Task(s)	Student/Teacher Conferring
Exit slip after focus lesson: "Name two important things you learned from this lesson." Practice with functions on www.mathground.com/FunctionMachine.html. Problem set 12.7 (p. 567) for homework * Select one problem and write an explanation for how you arrived at the solution.	Meet with students to discuss one or more of the following: 1. Written explanation of problem from homework problem set 2. Status of collaborative poster on functions 3. Status of independent project on graphs in everyday life

Assessment	
Formative	**Summative**
Exit slip	End-of-chapter quiz on functions
Products from guided instruction	Short essay on essential question: You and your classmates have
Homework	created function machines and graphs that do a variety of things.
Collaborative poster	Why do you think functions and relations are represented in dif-
	ferent ways? Use concepts from previous units as well as this one
	to support your answer. Include examples.

Source: Michael Soriano, San Diego, CA. Used by permission.

controller. This item is familiar to his students, and he further activates their prior knowledge by describing its use in a popular video game. He then displays an interactive math Web site using a laptop and data projector. The Web site features a game using a function machine. He shows the students how inputting a number will reveal a corresponding output. He then inputs numbers into the machine, thinking aloud as he first recognizes a pattern and then determines the function. After modeling his thinking several times, he shows his students how the game works and tells them that they will all have an opportunity to do the same on the classroom computers.

The following day, he reads aloud a picture book, *Two of Everything* (Hong, 1993), based on a Chinese folktale about a magic pot that duplicates anything that goes into it. As he reads, he models his understanding of the text and shares his thinking with students. After reading the book, he tells his students that they will turn this folktale into a series of equations using functions.

Guided Instruction

Mr. Soriano has planned several guided instruction lessons because he doesn't do the majority of his teaching in whole groups. He knows that time spent with smaller groups of students yields great rewards for him because he can be much more precise. His first guided lesson is whole group because he wants them to begin to make connections between the conceptual understandings he has built and the more formal language of mathematics. Displaying a T-chart of input (x) and output (y) variables, he asks students to record the chart in their math journals and then begin to think about how they will solve for the function. He guides their thinking, scaffolding through prompts and cues about previously learned knowledge, such as setting up an equation. Once they have solved it, he finishes with a formal explanation of the mathematical concepts they have just used.

Guided instruction continues the following day with Mr. Soriano meeting with small groups as they develop a similar equation for the situation in the story he has just read aloud. He asks each student to think aloud as they set up the equation. He doesn't need long to meet with them for this task, but it is important to him because this is the first time he will get to witness how individual students apply mathematical reasoning. He listens for misconceptions and makes a note about whom he will meet with again the following day for further guided instruction. He will implement another guided instruction lesson on graphing functions. The students have previously learned about domain and range, but he knows that novice mathematicians are less flexible in their thinking and are not always able to link background knowledge with new concepts. He wants them to understand that information can be represented in more than one way and wants to ensure that they visualize the function itself, not just the table. He will also reserve time later in the week to meet with students who had a significant number of errors on their homework.

Collaborative Learning

Knowing that collaborative learning is going on at the same time as guided instruction, Mr. Soriano has designed a series of activities that will take place over the next two days. He knows that initial collaborative learning must be easy enough for students to complete together, so he has them work in teams on the classroom computers using the same Web site he demonstrated during his focus lesson. They will bring functions they designed on the Web site to the guided instruction lesson on graphing so that they can use their examples to create new graphs. Other collaborative learning activities will include peer problem solving using problems from the textbook and a collaborative poster of a function machine that performs a real-world task. The poster task includes a graph, further extending their understanding of the different ways in which functions and relations are represented.

Concurrent Activities

Mr. Soriano always has overlapping projects going on in his math class. He is strategic in extending previously learned concepts into new units to further solidify the connections across the content. Therefore, his independent project due dates are often a week or so after the unit of study has ended so that students will continue to remain in contact with the material. In this case, they are continuing an independent learning assignment from the previous unit on graphing.

Independent Practice Tasks

Repetition and reinforcement are key to long-term retention of concepts and skills, so Mr. Soriano has chosen three independent practice tasks: an exit slip after the first day of instruction on what they learned, a problem set assigned for homework, and an additional requirement that they select one problem and write an explanation of their problem-solving process. This approach gives him further insight into who understands the concepts and who is still at the level of completing algorithms without understanding the underlying math principles.

Conferring

Mr. Soriano also knows that he needs to stay in close communication with his students because so much of their future learning this semester will build on the concepts learned now. He has identified three possible topics to discuss with each student and will meet briefly with each of them. These conferences don't take long, and he rotates through the class to informally confer with each student, making quick notes about their conversations for future reference.

Formative and Summative Assessments

Mr. Soriano has designed an instructional plan that yields several formative assessments, including exit slips, products from the guided instruction lessons, homework, and the collaborative poster. This combination provides him with the variety and authenticity he seeks in good assessment, and he communicates strongly to his students that math isn't just about "getting the right answers." His summative assessments include an end-of-chapter test from the teacher's guide accompanying the textbook series and a short essay addressing the essential question.

What to Look for in a Gradual Release of Responsibility Classroom

As schools and districts implement the gradual release model in their classrooms, it is important to identify indicators. As with Understanding by Design, identifying end results and determining acceptable evidence is essential to achieve desired outcomes (Wiggins & McTighe, 2005). Here are some indicators that coaches and administrators may use as they support teachers in developing a gradual release of responsibility framework.

Focus Lessons
- The teacher establishes the purpose for the lesson.
- Both content and language goals are established.
- The teacher uses "I" statements to model thinking.
- Questioning is used to scaffold instruction, not to interrogate students.

• The lesson includes a decision frame for when to use the skill or strategy.

• The lesson builds metacognitive awareness, especially indicators of success.

• Focus lessons move to guided instruction, not immediately to independent learning.

Guided Instruction

• Small-group arrangements are evident.

• Grouping changes throughout the semester.

• The teacher plays an active role in guided instruction, not just circulating and assisting individual students.

• A dialogue occurs between students and the teacher as they begin to apply the skill or strategy.

• The teacher uses cues and prompts to scaffold understanding when a student makes an error and does not immediately tell the student the correct answer.

Collaborative Learning

• Small-group arrangements are evident.

• Grouping changes throughout the semester.

• The teacher has modeled concepts that students need to complete collaborative tasks.

• Students have received guided instruction of the concepts needed to complete collaborative tasks.

Independent Learning

• Students have received focus lessons, guided instruction, and collaborative learning experiences related to concepts needed to complete independent tasks.

• Independent tasks extend beyond practice to application and extension of new knowledge.

• The teacher meets with individual students for conferencing about the independent learning tasks.

Questions to Ask

Determining where to begin in implementing a gradual release of responsibility framework can be daunting, particularly in knowing where to begin. We have developed these guiding questions to help integrate this approach into your instructional design.

Have I Modeled Things I Expect Students to Do Independently?

Many teachers may assume that collaborative and independent learning will take care of itself, yet we have discovered that explicit direction in collaborative and independent learning is the linchpin to a successful gradual release of responsibility classroom. We devote some time each class period during the first 10 days of the school year or semester to building the capacity of our students to work collaboratively and independently. We provide direct instruction through focus lessons on the tasks they will need to do, for example, using the classroom computers, writing responses to RAFT prompts, moving into collaborative groups, and completing independent reading assignments.

After we introduce each activity, we divide the students into groups so they can apply it. For example, after we have taught two collaborative learning activities, we split the class in half and ask each group to complete the task, and then switch. We spend our time circulating and assisting, monitoring behavior and redirecting students who are off task. As we introduce new collaborative and independent tasks, we further subdivide the class. Once we have taught the major tasks, including routines and procedures, we then introduce guided instruction into the mix. Only when students have been properly prepared for collaborative and independent learning can you count on having the (relatively) uninterrupted time you'll need for small-group guided instruction.

Do I Have the Materials I Need to Engage My Students?

This question relates to differentiated instruction, as you'll discover that your students need a range of materials to learn the content. The textbook is a great resource, but it is not the only item they should have. Bookmark Web sites on your classroom computer, and talk to your school librarian about the hidden treasures that are tucked away somewhere. We have worked at schools where grade levels assemble specialized materials and place them in labeled boxes for checkout. The resource kits are great because they encourage all of us to dig out materials we use only once a year. You may find that you need multiple copies of the same materials, such as file folder games for young children or storage bags of math manipulatives. Elementary schools are fortunate in being able to draw many family volunteers to complete these projects. If you are working at a middle or high school, consider promoting this practice as a community service project for an adolescent or young adult who is fulfilling requirements for a scholarship, diploma, or degree.

Are There Times That I Become the "Manager" and Not the Teacher? Can I Move These Tasks from Whole Class to Collaborative Learning?

We raised this point in the collaborative learning chapter, and it bears repeating. Pay attention to the times when you are not instructing but just managing—for example, showing a film in class, supervising independent work, or watching students as they read an assignment. Are you walking up and down the aisles, hushing students as you go? These behaviors are red flags that you have become a manager, not a teacher. Consider recasting some of these activities as collaborative tasks, and recognize that the time you need to instruct small groups of students is already there, just not being used.

Are Independent Learning Tasks Meaningful Applications of Content Learned in the Class?

We all vowed in our teacher preparation programs that we would never be one of *those* teachers who gave their students lots of busywork as a way to maintain order (meaning silence) in the classroom. We're not discounting the importance of independent work—we hope we have made a case that it is a critical component of a gradual release model. Rather, we are challenging the quality of what is traditionally used for independent work. Problem sets and questions at the end of the chapter are rarely engaging enough to keep most learners motivated. These practice-level tasks can be made more interesting by shifting them to the collaborative learning phase, where students now get an opportunity to use the social and academic language they need to support their own learning. Independent work should challenge learners to use content knowledge to synthesize and evaluate. These levels of Bloom's taxonomy are rarely attained through the traditional independent learning assignments mentioned here. Wilson and Cutting (2001) describe learning advancement in this way:

> *Finding out* (knowledge and comprehension levels)
> *Sorting out* (application and analysis levels)
> *Speaking out* (synthesis and evaluation levels) (p. 24)

All of these levels of understanding are important, but synthesis and evaluation are especially important to creating lasting understanding. If the independent learning tasks that students are completing are clumping up at the "finding out" and "sorting out" levels, to the exclusion of "speaking out" opportunities, then it is a signal that students can be shifted to focus lessons, guided instruction, or collaborative learning phases.

Have I Taught the Routines and Procedures Necessary for Students to Work in a Gradual Release Classroom?

This question is closely related to the first one regarding modeling independent tasks. Routines and procedures are essential in any classroom, regardless of the age of the students. Every classroom should have clear routines for retrieving and putting away supplies, turning in completed work, and asking for help, to name a few regular tasks. Other useful routines and procedures include the following:

• Schedules for collaborative learning and guided instruction groups
• Transitions between whole-group and small-group learning
• Monitoring of noise level in the classroom
• Closure at the end of class, including putting materials away, moving furniture, and giving homework assignments

Conclusion

The implementation of a gradual release of responsibility model of instruction is not accomplished overnight, but it can be successfully done over time. The recursive and iterative nature of this framework falls into place with experience in planning. This approach complements other research-based programs, especially differentiated instruction and backward planning. It is wise to consider the routines and procedures that students will need to know, and then dedicate some time each day to providing instruction on how to work collaboratively and independently. This approach will make the introduction of guided instruction much smoother, because students will already know what is expected from them when the teacher isn't standing in front of them.

As you prepare to close this book (and, we hope, to share it with a friend), reconsider how you learn. Think about the things you're good at and how you became good. Can you see the gradual release of responsibility model in your own learning? Can you see this approach resulting in better outcomes for students? The responsibility is now yours—enjoy!

References

Aldrich, C. (2005). *Learning by doing: A comprehensive guide to simulations, computer games, and pedagogy in e-learning and other educational experiences.* San Francisco: Jossey-Bass.

Alvermann, D. E., & Boothby, P. R. (1986). Children's transfer of graphic organizer instruction. *Reading Psychology, 7*(2), 87–100.

Anderson, N. J. (2002). The role of metacognition in second language teaching and learning. ERIC Clearinghouse on Language and Linguistics. Retrieved March 30, 2007, from http://www.cal.org/resources/digest/0110anderson.html

Angelo, T. A. (1991). Ten easy pieces: Assessing higher learning in four dimensions. *Classroom Research: Early Lessons from Success, 46,* 17–31.

Atkin, B. (2000). *Voices from the fields: Children of migrant farmworkers tell their stories.* New York: Little, Brown.

Bandura, A. (1965). Influence of models' reinforcement contingencies on the acquisition of imitative responses. *Journal of Personality and Social Psychology, 1,* 589–595.

Bandura, A. (1977). *Social learning theory.* Englewood Cliffs, NJ: Prentice Hall.

Beckman, M. (1990). Collaborative learning: Preparation for the workplace and democracy. *College Teaching, 38*(4), 128–133.

Benjamin, A. (2002). *Differentiated instruction: A guide for middle and high school teachers.* Larchmont, NY: Eye on Education.

Bennett, N., & Cass, A. (1988). The effects of group composition on group interactive processes and pupil understanding. *British Educational Research Journal, 15,* 19–32.

Black, P., & Wiliam, D. (1998). Assessment and classroom learning. *Assessment in Education, 5*(1), 7–74.

Bomer, R. (1999). Conferring with struggling readers: The test of our craft, courage, and hope. *New Advocate, 12*(1), 21–38.

Borzak, L. (Ed.). (1981). *Field study: A source book for experiential learning.* Thousand Oaks, CA: Sage.

Brochmann, H. (2007). *Iteration and recursion.* Retrieved April 2, 2007, from http://www.members.shaw.ca/FLYAWAYTOO/math/Recursion/Recur-1.00.html

Brookfield, S. D. (1995). *Becoming a critically reflective teacher.* San Francisco: Jossey-Bass.

Bruchac, J. (2001). *Sacajawea.* New York: Scholastic.

Camp, D. (2006). *Pairing fiction and nonfiction: Strategies to build comprehension in the content areas.* New York: Scholastic.

Candy, P. C. (1991). *Self-direction for lifelong learning.* San Francisco: Jossey-Bass.

Cazden, C. B. (1988). *Classroom discourse: The language of teaching and learning.* Portsmouth, NH: Heinemann.

Clay, M. M. (2000). *Running records for classroom teachers.* Portsmouth, NH: Heinemann.

Cleary, B. (1996). *A girl from Yamhill: A memoir.* New York: HarperTrophy.

Clements-Davis, G. L., & Ley, T. C. (1991). Thematic preorganizers and the reading comprehension of tenth-grade world literature students. *Reading Research & Instruction, 31*(1), 43–53.

Coleman, M. R., & Gallagher, J. J. (1995). Middle schools and their impact on talent development. *Middle School Journal, 26,* 47–56.

Covey, S. R. (2004). *The seven habits of highly effective people: Powerful lessons in personal change.* New York: Free Press.

Daniels, H. (2001). *Literature circles: Voice and choice in book clubs and reading groups.* York, ME: Stenhouse.

Daniels, H. (2006). What's the next big thing with literature circles? *Voices from the Middle, 13*(4), 10–15.

Denenberg, B. (1990). *Stealing home: The story of Jackie Robinson.* New York: Scholastic.

Diaz-Lefebvre, R. (2004). Multiple intelligences, learning for understanding, and creative assessment: Some pieces to the puzzle of learning. *Teachers College Record, 106,* 49–57.

Dick, W., Carey, L., & Carey, J. O. (2001). *The systematic design of instruction* (5th ed.). New York: Addison Wesley Longman.

Dodge, B. (1998). *Schools, skills and scaffolding on the Web.* Retrieved July 6, 2006, from http://edweb.sdsu.edu/people/bdodge/scaffolding.html

Dodge, B. J. (n.d.) *FOCUS: Five rules for writing a great WebQuest.* Retrieved March 31, 2007, at http://www.webquest.futuro.usp.br/artigos/textos_outros-bernie1.html

Duffy, G. G. (2003). *Explaining reading: A resource for teaching concepts, skills, and strategies.* New York: Guilford.

Duffy, G. G., Roehler, L. R., & Rackliffe, G. (1986). How teachers' instructional talk influences students' understanding of lesson content. *Elementary School Journal, 87*(1), 3–16.

Duke, N. K., & Pearson, P. D. (2002). Effective practices for developing reading comprehension. In A. E. Farstup & S. J. Samuels (Eds.), *What research has to say about reading instruction* (pp. 205–242). Newark, DE: International Reading Association.

Farmer, D. (1994). *Meeting the needs of gifted students in the regular classroom.* Sydney: Commonwealth of Australia.

Fisher, D. (2004). Setting the "opportunity to read" standard: Resuscitating the SSR program in an urban high school. *Journal of Adolescent & Adult Literacy, 48,* 138–150.

Fisher, D., & Frey, N. (2007a). *Checking for understanding: Formative assessment techniques for your classroom.* Alexandria, VA: Association for Supervision and Curriculum Development.

Fisher, D., & Frey, N. (2007b). *Improving adolescent literacy: Content area strategies at work* (2nd ed.) Upper Saddle River, NJ: Merrill Prentice Hall.

Fisher, D., & Frey, N. (2007c). *Scaffolded writing instruction: Teaching with a gradual-release framework.* New York: Scholastic.

Fisher, D., Frey, N., & Williams, D. (2002). Seven literacy strategies that work. *Educational Leadership, 60*(3), 70–73.

Flood, J., Lapp, D., Flood, S., & Nagel, G. (1992). Am I allowed to group? Using flexible patterns for effective instruction. *The Reading Teacher, 45,* 608–615.

Fountas, I. C., & Pinnell, G. S. (1996). *Guided reading: Good first teaching for all children.* Portsmouth, NH: Heinemann.

Frank, A. (1993). *Anne Frank: The diary of a young girl.* New York: Bantam Books.

Frey, N., & Fisher, D. (2006). *Language arts workshop: Purposeful reading and writing instruction.* Upper Saddle River, NJ: Merrill/Prentice Hall.

Fullan, M., Hill, P., & Crévola, C. (2006). *Breakthrough.* Thousand Oaks, CA: Corwin.

Fulwiler, T., & Young, A. (1982). *Language connections: Writing and reading across the curriculum.* Urbana, IL: National Council of Teachers of English.

Gallant, R. A. (2000). *Comets, asteroids, and meteorites.* New York: Benchmark Books.

Ganci, C. (2003). *Chief: The life of Peter J. Ganci, a New York City firefighter.* New York: Orchard.

Gardner, H. (2006). *Multiple intelligences: New horizons.* New York: Perseus Books.

Gersten, R., & Baker, S. (2000). What we know about effective instructional practices for English language learners. *Exceptional Children, 66,* 454–470.

Goldman, S. R., & Pellegrino, J. (1986). Microcomputer: Effective drill and practice. *Academic Therapy, 22*(2), 133–140.

Graff, G., & Birkenstein, C. (2006). *They say/I say: The moves that matter in academic writing.* New York: Norton.

Graves, M. F., & Fitzgerald, J. (2003). Scaffolding reading experiences for multilingual classrooms. In G. G. García (Ed.), *English learners: Reaching the highest level of English literacy* (pp. 96–124). Newark, DE: International Reading Association.

Guzzetti, B. J., Synder, T. E., Glass, G. V., & Gamas, W. S. (1993). Promoting conceptual change in science: A comparative meta-analysis of instructional interventions from reading education and science education. *Reading Research Quarterly, 28,* 116–159.

Heuser, D. (2000). Reworking the workshop for math and science. *Educational Leadership, 58*(1), 34–37.

Hill, J. D., & Flynn, K. M. (2006). *Classroom instruction that works with English language learners.* Alexandria, VA: Association for Supervision and Curriculum Development.

Holdaway, D. (1979). *The foundations of literacy.* New York: Scholastic.

Hong, L. T. (1993). *Two of everything.* New York: Whitman.

Ivey, G., & Broaddus, K. (2001). "Just plain reading": A survey of what makes students want to read in middle school classrooms. *Reading Research Quarterly, 36,* 350-377.

Johnson, D. W., & Johnson, R. (1999). *Learning together and alone: Cooperative, competitive, and individualistic learning* (2nd ed.). Boston: Allyn & Bacon.

Johnson, D. W., Johnson, R. T., & Smith, K. (1991). *Active learning: Cooperation in the college classroom.* Edina, MN: Interaction Book Company.

Kellough, R. D., & Kellough, N. G. (1999). *Secondary school teaching: A guide to methods and resources.* Upper Saddle River, NJ: Prentice Hall.

Kesten, C. (1987). *Independent learning.* Regina, Canada: Saskatchewan Education.

Kolb, D. A. (1984). *Experiential learning.* Englewood Cliffs, NJ: Prentice Hall.

Kolb, D. A., & Fry, R. (1975). Toward an applied theory of experiential learning. In C. Cooper (Ed.), *Studies of group process* (pp. 33–57). New York: Wiley.

Krull, K. (2003). *Harvesting hope: The story of César Chávez.* San Diego, CA: Harcourt.

Krull, K. (2004). *A woman for president: The story of Victoria Woodhull.* New York: Walker.

Kucan, L., & Beck, I. L. (1997). Thinking aloud and reading comprehension research: Inquiry, instruction, and social interaction. *Review of Educational Research, 67,* 271–299.

LaBerge, D. I., & Samuels, S. J. (1974). Toward a theory of automatic information processing in reading. *Cognitive Psychology, 6,* 293–323.

Levstik, L., & Barton, K. (1997). *Doing history: Investigating with children in elementary and middle schools.* Mahwah, NJ: Erlbaum.

Lewis, M., Bergon, F., & Clark, W. (2003). *The journals of Lewis and Clark.* New York: Penguin.

Marzano, R. J., Pickering, D. J., & Pollock, J. E. (2001). *Classroom instruction that works: Research-based strategies for increasing student achievement.* Alexandria, VA: Association for Supervision and Curriculum Development.

Mason, D. A., & Good, T. L. (1993). Effects of two-group and whole-class teaching on regrouped elementary students' mathematics achievement. *American Educational Research Journal, 30,* 328–360.

McInnerney, J., & Roberts, T. S. (2005). Collaborative and cooperative learning. In *The encyclopedia of distance learning: Volume 1. Online learning and technologies* (pp. 269–276). Hershey, PA: Information Science Publishing.

Mooney, M. (1988). *Developing life-long readers.* Wellington, New Zealand: Learning Media.

Moore, D. W., & Readence, J. E. (1984). A quantitative and qualitative review of graphic organizer research. *Journal of Educational Research, 78*(1), 11–17.

Mulryan, C. (1995). Fifth and sixth graders' involvement and participation in cooperative small groups in mathematics. *Elementary School Journal, 95*(4), 297–310.

Nathan, M. J., & Petrosino, A. (2003). Expert blind spot among preservice teachers. *American Educational Research Journal, 40,* 905–928.

National Council of Teachers of Mathematics. (2000). *Principles and standards for school mathematics.* Retrieved March 31, 2007, from http://standards. nctm.org/document/chapter2/assess.htm

National Research Council. (2006). *America's lab report: Investigations in high school science.* Washington, DC: National Academies Press.

National Research Council, Division of Behavioral and Social Sciences and Education. (2005). *How students learn: History, mathematics, and science in the classroom.* Washington, DC: National Academies Press.

Naylor, P. R. (1991). *Shiloh.* New York: Atheneum.

O'Brien, T. C., & Moss, A. (2004). What's basic in mathematics? Rote memorization of arithmetic "facts" isn't as important as making sense of math concepts and applying them to the everyday world. *Principal, 84*(2), 25–27.

Oczkus, L. D. (2003). *Reciprocal teaching at work: Strategies for improving reading comprehension.* Newark, DE: International Reading Association.

Opitz, M. F., & Rasinski, T. (1998). *Good-bye round robin: 25 effective oral reading strategies.* Portsmouth, NH: Heinemann.

Palincsar, A. S., & Brown, A. L. (1984). Reciprocal teaching of comprehension-fostering and comprehension-monitoring activities. *Cognition and Instruction, 1,* 117–175.

Parker, S. (2005). *Electricity.* New York: DK.

PBS. (2007). Elements of a slide. *Nova: Avalanche!* Retrieved March 31, 2007, from http://www.pbs.org/wgbh/nova/avalanche/elements.html

Pearson, P. D., & Gallagher, G. (1983). The gradual release of responsibility model of instruction. *Contemporary Educational Psychology, 8,* 112–123.

Petrie, K. (2003). *The food pyramid.* Edina, MN: Abdo.

Piaget, J. (1952). *The origins of intelligence in children.* New York: Norton.

Pilgreen, J. (2000). *The SSR handbook: How to organize and manage a sustained silent reading program.* Portsmouth, NH: Heinemann.

Pincus, A. R. H. (2005). What's a teacher to do? Navigating the worksheet curriculum. *The Reading Teacher, 59,* 75–79.

Race, P. (1996). *A fresh look at independent learning.* Retrieved April 2, 2007, from http://www.city.londonmet.ac.uk/deliberations/eff.learning/indep. html

Raphael, T. E., Highfield, K., & Au, K. H. (2006). *QAR now: A powerful and practical framework that develops comprehension and higher-level thinking in all students.* New York: Scholastic.

Raphael, T. E., Pardo, L. S., & Highfield, K. (2002). *Book club: A literature-based curriculum* (2nd ed.). Lawrence, MA: Small Planet Communications.

Rigby. (2004). *Dad.* San Diego, CA: Harcourt.

Rogers, C. (1969). *Freedom to learn: A view of what education might become.* Columbus, OH: Merrill.

Ryan, P. M. (2000). *Esperanza rising.* New York: Scholastic.

Santa, C., & Havens, L. (1995). *Creating independence through student-owned strategies: Project CRISS.* Dubuque, IA: Kendall-Hunt.

Sapon-Shevin, M. (2007). *Widening the circle: The power of inclusive classrooms.* Boston: Beacon.

Saskatchewan Education. (n.d.). *Understanding the common essential learnings.* Regina, Canada: Author. Retrieved March 31, 2007, from http://www. sasked.gov.sk.ca/docs/policy/cels/el7.html

Slavin, R. E. (1980). Cooperative learning. *Review of Educational Research, 50,* 315–342.

Slavin, R. E. (1983). When does cooperative learning increase student achievement? *Psychological Bulletin, 94,* 429–445.

Stevens, R. J., & Slavin, R. E. (1995). Effectiveness of a cooperative learning approach in reading and writing on academically handicapped and non-handicapped students. *Elementary School Journal, 95,* 241–262.

Summers, J. J. (2006). Effects of collaborative learning in math on sixth graders' individual goal orientations from a socioconstructivist perspective. *Elementary School Journal, 106,* 273–290.

Summers, S. (2004). Museums as resources for science teachers. *Science Scope, 27*(9), 28–29.

Swearingen, R. (2002). *A primer: Diagnostic, formative, and summative assessment.* Retrieved April 2, 2007, from http://www.mmrwsjr.com/assessment. htm

Tate, M. L. (2003). *Worksheets don't grow dendrites.* Thousand Oaks, CA: Corwin Press.

Tomlinson, C. A. (2001). *How to differentiate instruction in mixed-ability classrooms.* Alexandria, VA: Association for Supervision and Curriculum Development.

Tomlinson, C. A. (2003). *Differentiation in practice: A resource guide for differentiating instruction.* Alexandria, VA: Association for Supervision and Curriculum Development.

Totten, S., Sills, T., Digby, A., & Russ, P. (1991). *Cooperative learning: A guide to research.* New York: Garland.

University of Minnesota, Center for Teaching and Learning. (2006). *Designing smart lectures*. Retrieved March 30, 2007, from http://www1.umn.edu/ohr/teachlearn/tutorials/lectures/overview.html

Vygotsky, L. S. (1962). *Thought and language*. Cambridge, MA: MIT Press.

Vygotsky, L. S. (1978). *Mind in society*. Cambridge, MA: Harvard University Press.

Webb, N. M. (1982). Student interaction and learning in small groups. *Review of Educational Research, 52,* 421–445.

Wiggins, G., & McTighe, J. (2005). *Understanding by design* (2nd ed.). Alexandria, VA: Association for Supervision and Curriculum Development.

Wilhelm, J. (2001). *Improving comprehension with think-aloud strategies: Modeling what good readers do*. New York: Scholastic.

Willis, J. (2005). Sharpen kids' memory to raise test scores. *Education Digest, 70* (7), 20–24.

Wilson, J., & Cutting, L. (2001). *Contracts for independent learning: Engaging students in the middle years*. Melbourne, Australia: Curriculum Corporation.

Wood, D., Bruner, J. S., & Ross, G. (1976). The role of tutoring and problem solving. *Journal of Child Psychology and Psychiatry, 17,* 89–100.

Yeh, S. S. (2006). High-stakes testing: Can rapid assessment reduce the pressure? *Teachers College Record, 108,* 621–661.

Index

ability grouping, 40, 64–65
accountability, individual and group, 66–67, 83–84
Aronson, Elliot, 80
assessment, formative
    in collaborative learning, 83–84
    in focus lessons, 37–38
    in guided instruction, 43–46, 58–60
    implementing in model, 123, 127
    in independent learning tasks, 105–107
assessment, purposes and types, 44–45
assessment, summative, 107–109
authenticity, assessment, 107
authentic voice, 32
automaticity, 81–82

Ball Foundation, 114
Bandura, Albert, 3
Bloom's taxonomy, 131–132
book clubs, 73–76
Bruner, J., 3

Choice Literacy, 101–103

clarifying, 68–69
collaborative learning
    about, 7–9, 12–13, 62–65
    avoiding managing, 130–131
    features of, 65–67
    formative assessment and, 83–84
    implementing, 125–126, 128
    instructional strategies for, 67–81
    jigsaw, 80–81
    labs and simulations, 76–80
    listening/viewing stations, 70–72
    literature circles/book clubs, 73–76
    reciprocal teaching, 67–70
    sample lesson plan, 122
    skills practice, 81–83
    visual displays, 72–73
conditional dimension of learning, 24
conferring, 101–105
content area expertise, 32
content differentiation, 46–47
content domain, 21
crystal ball prompt, 100

declarative dimension of learning, 24
demonstration, 26–28

differentiated instruction, 6, 41, 46–48, 113

direct explanation, 24–25

Dodge, Bernie, 43

entry slips prompt, 97

essential questions, 115

exit slip prompt, 100

exit writing, 38, 100

experiential learning, 89–90

expert blind spots, 32

expertise, 2

face-to-face interactions, 66

focus lessons
  about, 4–5, 17
  formative assessments in, 37–38
  implementation, 115, 124, 127–128
  instructional strategies for, 22–37
  key features, 21–22
  metacognitive awareness in, 22, 28–30
  modeling in, 22, 23–28, 129–130
  public problem solving, 30–31
  sample lesson plan, 120
  shared reading, 33–34
  things to avoid during, 17–20
  think-alouds in, 23, 31–33
  write-alouds, 35–37

formative assessments
  in collaborative learning, 83–84
  in focus lessons, 37–38
  in guided instruction, 45–46, 58–60
  in independent learning tasks, 105–107

frames, 53–54

gradual release of responsibility model
  about, 2–4
  collaborative learning, 7–9, 12–13, 62–85
  focus lessons, 4–5, 17–38
  guided instruction, 6–7, 39–61

gradual release of responsibility model (continued)
  independent learning tasks, 9–10, 12, 86–109

gradual release of responsibility model—implementation
  assessments, 123, 127
  collaborative learning, 122, 125–126, 128
  conferring, 126–127
  and differentiated instruction, 113
  focus lesson, 115, 120, 124, 127–128
  guided instruction, 121, 124–125, 128
  guiding questions for, 129–132
  independent learning tasks, 126, 128–129
  indicators for correct implementation, 127–129
  iterativeness of, 111–112
  planning tool for, 114–115, 116–119
  recursiveness of, 111
  and Understanding by Design, 113–114

graphic organizers, 72

grouping, 40, 46, 64–65

group processing, 67

group work, 64

guided instruction
  about, 6–7, 39–40, 60–61
  features of, 41–48
  formative assessments with, 58–60
  guided reading, 48–51, 58
  guided writing, 51–54, 59
  implementation, 124–125, 128
  instructional strategies for, 48–58
  misconception analysis, 56–58, 59
  sample lesson plan, 121
  student think-alouds, 54–56, 59, 60

guided reading, 48–51, 58

guided writing, 51–54, 59

independent learning centers, 91–93

independent learning tasks
about, 9–10, 12, 86–89, 109
assessments in, 105–109
conferring, 101–105
features, 89–91
implementation, 126, 128–129
independent learning centers,
91–93
independent reading, 93, 97–99
instructional strategies for, 91–105
meaningful, 131–132
routines and procedures for, 132
sustained silent reading, 93–94,
95, 106
writing to prompts, 97–101, 107
independent reading, 93, 97–99
instructional goals, 5
instructional strategies
conferring, 101–105
guided reading, 48–51, 58
guided writing, 51–54, 59
independent learning centers,
91–93
independent reading, 93, 97–99
jigsaw, 80–81
labs and simulations, 76–80
listening/viewing stations, 70–72
literature circles/book clubs,
73–76
metacognitive awareness, 22,
28–30, 33, 56
misconception analysis, 56–58, 59
modeling, 3, 4–5, 23–28, 129–130
public problem solving, 30–31
reciprocal teaching, 67–70
shared reading, 33–34
sustained silent reading, 93–94,
95, 106
student think-alouds, 54–56, 59, 60
think-alouds, 23, 31–33
visual displays, 72–73
write-alouds, 35–37
writing to prompts, 97–101, 107
interdependence, positive, 66
interpersonal skills, 67

jigsaw, 80–81

labs, 76–78
language domain, 21
learning
defined, 1
four dimensions of, 24
poor classroom models for, 10–13
Rogers' principles of, 90–91
lectures, 20
listening/viewing stations, 70–72
literacy across curriculum, 115
literature circles, 73–76

materials, instructional, 130
McTighe, Jay, 112, 113–114
metacognitive awareness, 22, 28–30,
33, 56
misconception analysis, 56–58, 59
modeling
about, 3, 4–5, 22, 23–24
demonstration, 26–28
direct explanation, 24–25
importance, 129–130
Mooney, Margaret, 39
multiple intelligences, 89

Northview (Grand Rapids, MI) Public
Schools, 114

partner talk, 37–38
peer learning, 3. *See also* collaborative learning
Piaget, Jean, 2
practice, skills, 81–83
predicting, 69
prescriptive teaching, 16, 40
procedural dimension of learning, 24
process differentiation, 47
product differentiation, 47
production scaffolds, 43, 44
products, single *vs.* multiple, 7
public problem solving, 30–31
purpose for learning, establishing,
21–22

questioning, 68

Race, Phil, 86–87
RAFT prompt, 100–101
reading, guided, 48–51, 58
reading, independent, 93, 97–99
reading, sustained silent (SSR),
 93–94, 95, 106
reading aloud, 20
reading inventories, informal, 58–59
reception scaffolds, 43, 44
reciprocal teaching, 8, 67–70
reflective dimension of learning, 24
reliability, assessment, 108–109
Ross, G., 3
rote memorization, 81–82, 89
rubrics, self-assessment, 96, 98–99

scaffolding, 41–44
science education, 76–78
Sevenbergen, Sheri, 96
shared reading, 33–34

simulations, 78–80
Simulations International, 78
skills practice, 81–83
small-group skills, 67
social domain, 21
Soriano, Michael, 115
subject-matter knowledge, 32
summarizing, 68

summative assessment, 107–109
sustained silent reading (SSR), 93–94,
 95, 106

teachers, conferring with, 101–105
templates, 53–54
think-alouds, student, 54–56, 59, 60
think-alouds, teacher, 23, 31–33
Tomlinson, Carol Ann, 112, 113
transformation scaffolds, 43, 44
transparency, in focus lessons, 17

Understanding by Design (UbD),
 113–114

validity, assessment, 108
variety, assessment, 107–108
visual displays, 72–73
volume, assessment, 108
Vygotsky, Lev, 2

WebQuest approach, 43
Wiggins, Grant, 112, 113–114
Wood, D., 3
worksheets, 86, 88
write-alouds, 35–37
writing, guided, 51–54, 59
writing to prompts, 97–101, 107

Yesterday's news prompt, 97

About the Authors

Douglas Fisher, PhD, is a professor of language and literacy education in the Department of Teacher Education at San Diego State University (SDSU), the co-director for the Center for the Advancement of Reading at the California State University Chancellor's office, and the past director of professional development for the City Heights Educational Collaborative. He is the recipient of an International Reading Association Celebrate Literacy Award as well as a Christa McAuliffe Award for Excellence in Teacher Education. He has published numerous articles on reading and literacy, differentiated instruction, and curriculum design as well as books such as *Creating Literacy-rich Schools for Adolescents* (with Gay Ivey), *Improving Adolescent Literacy: Strategies at Work* and *Checking for Understanding* (both with Nancy Frey), and *Language Learners in the English Classroom* (with Carol Rothenberg and Nancy Frey). He has taught a variety of courses in SDSU's teacher-credentialing program as well as graduate-level courses on English language development and literacy. A former early intervention specialist and language development specialist, he has also taught high school English, writing, and literacy development to public school students. He can be reached at dfisher@mail.sdsu.edu.

Nancy Frey, PhD, is an associate professor of literacy in the School of Teacher Education at San Diego State University. Before joining the university faculty, Nancy was a teacher in the Broward County (Florida) Public Schools, where she taught both general and special education students at the elementary and middle school levels. She later worked for the Florida Department of Education on a statewide project for supporting students with diverse learning needs in general education curriculum. She is a recipient of the Christa McAuliffe Award for Excellence in Teacher Education from the American Association of State Colleges and Universities. Her research interests include reading and literacy, assessment, intervention, and curriculum design. She has coauthored several books on literacy, including *Language Arts Workshop: Purposeful Reading and Writing Instruction* and *Reading for Information in Elementary School* (both with Doug Fisher). She teaches a variety of courses in SDSU's teacher-credentialing program on elementary and secondary literacy in content area instruction and supporting students with diverse learning needs. She can be reached at nfrey@mail.sdsu.edu.

Related ASCD Resources

Related ASCD Resources: Teaching

At the time of publication, the following ASCD resources were available (ASCD stock numbers appear in parentheses). For up-to-date information about ASCD resources, go to www.ascd.org.

Audiotapes

Instructional Approaches of Superior Teachers by Lloyd Campbell (#299202)

Putting Best Practices to Work on Behalf of Improving Student Learning by Kathleen Fitzpatrick (#298132)

Teaching for the 21st Century by Linda Darling-Hammond (#297247)

Mixed Media

Making School Improvement Happen with What Works in Schools: Teacher-Level Factors: An ASCD Action Tool by John L. Brown (#705054)

Teaching for Understanding: An ASCD Professional Inquiry Kit by Charlotte Danielson (#196212)

Print Products

Classroom Instruction That Works: Research-based Strategies for Increasing Student Achievement by Robert J. Marzano, Debra J. Pickering, and Jane E. Pollock *(#101010)*

Enhancing Professional Practice: A Framework for Teaching (2nd edition) by Charlotte Danielson *(#106034)*

Habits of Mind: A Developmental Series edited by Arthur L. Costa and Bena Kallick *(#100036)*

A Handbook for Classroom Instruction That Works by Robert J. Marzano, Jennifer S. Norford, Diane E. Paynter, Debra J. Pickering, and Barbara B. Gaddy *(#101041)*

Qualities of Effective Teachers (2nd edition) by James H. Stronge *(#105156)*

Videotapes

The How To Collection: Instruction That Promotes Learning (six 15-minute video programs on one 110-minute DVD) *(#606141)*

Library of Teaching Strategies Parts I & II (#614178)

A Visit to Classrooms of Effective Teachers (one 45-minute program with a comprehensive Viewer's Guide) (DVD: #605026; videotape: #405026)

What Works in Schools: School Factors with Robert J. Marzano (Tape 1: #403048)

What Works in Schools: Teacher Factors with Robert J. Marzano (Tape 2: #403049)

For more information: send e-mail to member@ascd.org; call 1-800-933-2723 or 703-578-9600 and press 2; send a fax to 703-575-5400; or write to Information Services, ASCD, 1703 N. Beauregard St., Alexandria, VA 22311-1714 USA.